Hungry to Be Happy

How I Lost and Found My Mind

Harry Averill

A catalogue record for this book is available from the National Library of New Zealand

IBSN 978-1-99-118670-6 (Paperback)

IBSN 978-1-99-118671-3 (eBook)

Cover artwork by Zonny @zonny.flow

Cover photograph by Jusy @whatisjusy

To Mum, for all you've contributed to this book, and all you've ever done for me.

"The mind is its own place, and in itself can make a heaven of Hell, a hell of Heaven."

John Milton: Paradise Lost

CONTENTS

INTRODUCTION 1

1. THE LINE IN THE SAND 4

2. CATCHING THE BUG 15

3. THE SLIPPERY SLOPE 30

4. RASH DECISIONS 42

5. THE FIRST SICK DAY 52

6. DANGEROUS TERRITORY 65

7. HITTING ROCK BOTTOM 80

8. TWO SIDES OF THE SAME COIN 86

9. FOUR WHITE WALLS 99

10. LIFE IN THE CAPITAL 115

11. DRAFTING SHEEP 131

12. FINDING THE SWITCH 146

13. SEEING THE LIGHT 159

14. HOME 183

15. FAKE IT TILL YOU MAKE IT 197

16. THE COMEBACK 212
17. PULLING THE FINGER 223
18. THE NEXT CHAPTER 239
THANKS 256
GETTING HELP 261

INTRODUCTION

This story nearly ended nine years ago, but it didn't. Pages continued to turn, and words continued to fill them.

I wouldn't say I'm religious, but I do believe things happen the way they were always meant to. I don't know why I survived my ordeal in the same way I don't know why I went through it in the first place. Things just happen, and I'm okay with not knowing why they happen the way they do.

What I do know, is that I wouldn't change a thing that happened to me. I may not have deserved to go through what I did, but having gone through it anyway, I sure as hell deserve the lessons it taught me. I deserve to know what I do now.

Nine years have passed since my story had its first dramatic twist, and with a bit of luck, it is still far from finished. Yet many chapters have already run their course, and with that, many lessons have already been learned. This book is a collection of the chapters I think are worth sharing.

I'll be the first to admit that this book won't be for everyone. Movies have age restrictions for a reason; at different stages of our lives, some stories are better off unheard. If you think delving into my journey through anorexia will do you more harm than good, I strongly encourage you to throw this thing at the nearest wall. This book may not be for you, and that's okay. Knowing your limits is a great strength, and throwing things at walls is a great feeling.

For the rest of you, I hope this book can be more than just a throwable object. Life can and should be awesome, but it can also turn to shit. If your life is awesome, I hope this book makes it more awesome or at least makes you appreciate how awesome you've got it. Just because life is good doesn't mean it can't be better, and you shouldn't have to lose your mind to appreciate the bliss of a healthy one.

Alternatively, your life might have turned to shit. Mental illness is just one of the ways this can happen, but it seems to be one that touches a lot of us. If you or someone close to you is tasting the shitty side of life, I hope you can find things in my story that can help you in yours. If nothing else, I hope this book gives you just that – hope, for its power is unparalleled.

Nine years ago, I didn't think I could ever be normal again, let alone what my life could one day become. Yet I've learned that no matter how far off track we wander, there is always a way back and that when we get there, there is always a way forward.

Bad things happen, but their effects on our stories do not need to be permanent. That's what my story has taught me. I hope it can teach you that too.

One

THE LINE IN THE SAND

As a kid, I was one of the lucky ones. Born in good health into a great family, I had two parents that loved each other and four highly involved, healthy grandparents. We didn't consider ourselves rich, but we were a long way off poor and as New Zealanders, there was never too much for us to worry about. Life was good.

I had two brothers, one two years older and one three years younger. Fighting with them was the closest I ever came to conflict, but as well as being my biggest rivals, they were also my best mates. As the middle brother, I won just as many fights as I lost, and of those I lost, they all built character. I wouldn't have had it any other way.

Home for us was on the east coast of the North Island, and my childhood was split between Gisborne and Hawke's Bay. It's an incredibly laid-back part of the country: the first place in the world to see the sun and a place where it always seems to shine. Shoes are considered optional, pyjamas are socially acceptable in public, and dirty elbows and knees are the ultimate badges of honour. I couldn't think of a better place to be a kid.

PlayStations and iPods were just starting to make their mark in the early 2000s, yet for my brothers and me, the outdoors always held on to their appeal. We built huts, rode bikes, and threw plenty of rocks at things we shouldn't have. There was a bit of fishing thrown in there, too, but using just a stick with bait tied to its end was never as effective as we'd hoped. The fish may have never made it to shore, but those days spent waiting for them will always be some of my favourites.

When it came to sport, I loved nothing more than getting stuck in the thick of it. Like most boys in New Zealand, I played rugby in the winter, cricket in the summer, and tennis whenever we could find enough balls in the garden. Going to school was an inconvenience amongst all of this, but I secretly never minded it too much and was always curious to learn new things. I even played the piano for a few years but stopped as soon as a mate told me it was lame.

I was just your typical, happy-go-lucky kid, and in the initial lottery of life, I don't think I could have done much better. I may not have always appreciated it at the time, but my life was bliss, and being inside my head was a great place to be. Then came high school. That's when everything started to change.

***

No matter who you are, starting high school is a big deal. Starting boarding school is an even bigger one. It was the most significant change in my life to date, and like most kids, I was desperate to get it right.

For me, though, it felt like more than just the start of something new, and how I approached things once I got there reflected that. In the context of my life, starting high school felt like a line in the sand: it was a beginning, but it was also an end. On one side of that line was my childhood and everything in my life that had gone before. On the other side was growing up, becoming a man, and building myself the kind of future I'd always hoped for. The way I saw it, high school was when my time as a kid ran out and growing up began.

As a kid, I knew I could shirk or stuff up as much as I liked, yet in the big scheme of things, none of it really mattered. No matter what I did or didn't do, my future would always remain intact. The meaning of life was to have fun, so my enjoyment could form the basis of almost every decision I made. I appreciated the value of hard work, but as a kid, my time to work hard was always ahead of me.

Once I started high school and crossed that line in the sand, I began living under a new set of rules. The way I saw it, that was when the things I did or didn't do started counting towards my future, so the long-term outcomes of my behaviour became relevant for the first time.

Under this kind of framework, I could no longer justify having the same approach to life that I had as a kid. From what I could understand, success was key to a happy future, yet there could be no gain without pain. High school was my one chance to set the trajectory of my life, so the more sacrifices I could make in those five years, the more successful – and eventually happy – I could be.

The last thing I wanted was to sell myself short, so whether I liked it or not, the fun and games of childhood would have to stop.

Such distinctions were ones I never needed to make, and looking back, I often wonder how they found their way into my head. Realistically, there were probably all sorts of influences there that I'll never be able to put a Freudian finger on. I'd always been ambitious, yet how ambition was able to fuel such a dramatic shift in approach at such a tender age is something I still can't understand.

What I do know, is that as a kid who wanted nothing more than to sit at the adults' table, these distinctions were ones that I was all too willing to accept. It may have been a grossly inaccurate interpretation of what it takes to grow up and be happy, but it made sense to me at the time, so I ran with it.

It was the first of many misconceptions I would develop that year – the first in a chain reaction of false beliefs that would eventually almost kill me.

***

By New Zealand standards, Napier Boys' High is a reasonably big school, with almost two hundred boarders and around twelve hundred students in total. Like most all-male high schools, it contains a mix of prepubescent boys, fully-grown men, and all sorts of strange creatures in between. I was glad to have a few hairs sprouting out of the usual locations of interest and a voice that dropped a couple of octaves when I tried hard enough. Aside from that, I can't have looked long out of the sandpit.

I was one of around forty others starting in the hostel that year and was lucky to know a handful of them from previous schools and sports teams. My older brother, Jack, had also been there for a couple of years, and I was lucky to have several cousins there, too.

Fortunately, these relatives all had the reputation of being reasonably good blokes, so sharing their last name was always more a blessing than a curse. I started a long way down the boarding school pecking order, but for a Year Nine, things definitely could have been worse.

When you start in the hostel, you spend a lot of time running, particularly in your first couple of weeks. The idea here is that running is a cheap and easy way to prevent boys from getting homesick. You're kept too busy to think about home, and once bedtime comes around, you're too exhausted to do anything but go straight to sleep. It's a genius strategy and, as far as I know, one that continues to this day.

Jack warned me of all this in advance, so I'd tried to maintain my fitness from the previous rugby season. It had been a particularly long and intense season, so when I arrived at the hostel, I happened to be fitter than most. This should have made all that running seem easy, but it didn't. As it turns out, being fit means nothing when you decide to push yourself to your limits.

A few minutes after saying goodbye to our parents, a housemaster asked the forty of us newbies to run a few laps of the field. This came as a surprise to most, but after getting the lowdown from Jack, I'd been psyching myself up for that moment for months.

I was overtly aware that – as of a few minutes ago – my childhood was over, which meant it was time to start turning my intentions into action. In the high-stakes life I now found myself in, this was essentially my debut. It was my first chance to prove my worth to those who matter, and with that in mind, I was determined to run harder than ever before.

I may not have won the race, but almost collapsing over the finish line felt like a success in itself.

Another way the hostel prevented us from getting homesick in those first couple of weeks was by banning our phones. The logic here was that if we couldn't ring our families and hear the voices of our beloved mothers and fathers, we were less likely to miss them.

Instead, we were encouraged to write letters home during prep each night. There wasn't much homework for us to do that early in the piece, so like most boys, I took their advice and started a bit of old-fashioned correspondence.

The following is one of the letters I managed to come up with during my first week and the chalk and cheese replies it generated from my Mum and Dad. Please excuse my vocabulary choices – I promise they were cool at the time.

To Mum, Dad, and Oscar,

We are in prep at the moment. We have just been playing rugby against the year 10s. That was sick. After you first left we went for a run around the field and went for a swim. On Tuesday us hostels went into the gym with all the dayboys and got put into our classes. I think I'm in the top class.

After school that day we went for a run along Marine Parade for 6.5km. I came 2nd and it was hot as. On Saturday we went to Cape Kidnappers. That was alright. We also had the road race which was a 4km run.

On Sunday we had the relay to Waimārama. I had to run an uphill bit which was pretty hard because I tried sprinting the whole way. We broke the record by 5 minutes which was mean. Then we went for a swim in the sea and got fish and chips.

The food has been nice but not as good as at home Mum. I have only eaten one of those muesli bars you gave me because I have been full as with all the tucker here. Overall everyone here is cool and I'm having a mean as time so far.

Happy birthday for tomorrow Mum but this probably won't get there in time.

The end.

Dear Harryboy!

I'm sitting in bed writing this, about to get up and head off for another day at work. Well, dying to know how you are getting on? I've texted Jack a few times but he doesn't give me much information! Can't wait till next Friday when I get to have you home for the 100 question grilling!

Oscar had the day at Granny and Papa's yesterday. I do believe he is actually missing you guys. Things are a bit quiet here so not a lot to report!

So proud of you for getting into the top class. Who else is in there I would know? How are all your other mates getting on? And who are you hanging out with? I would love to be a fly on the wall Harry! Make sure you text me on Wednesday when you get your phone back and I'll give you a ring.

Oh well, Dad's out of the shower now so better get up and have mine. Molly's just come and plonked herself on my bed!

Hope you have a great weekend, although it may have been and gone by the time you get this! Have fun! Love you lots and missing you.

All my love, Mum xoxo

Hello Harry,

How are you mate? It sounds like you are settling in very well which is great. It's strange not having you around every day but we are looking forward to seeing you next weekend! Anyway Harry, have a great week.

Love Dad

***

By all accounts, my time at Napier Boys' had gotten off to a great start. I'd made it into a good class, formed a solid group of mates, and even did alright in those notorious hostel running races. Naturally, I was stoked.

With my year starting so well, it felt as though my new approach to life was paying immediate dividends. At the time, I remember feeling like I'd discovered some kind of secret and wondered why I hadn't taken life more seriously before.

In just two weeks, so much in my life had changed, yet by adopting that 'no pain, no gain' mindset and trying my best at every opportunity, I'd also never felt more in control of my future. Everything I touched was turning to gold, and at a time when the stakes had never been higher, I felt like I was nailing it.

This reaffirmed every misconception I had about high school, growing up, and what it took to be successful. What were initially just thoughts were becoming actions, and what were initially just theories were becoming irrefutable truths. 2013 may have started well, but it was all downhill from there.

Two

CATCHING THE BUG

Running is a notoriously unenjoyable sport, and as a kid, I hated it with an absolute passion. I guess I liked the idea of pushing myself and the feeling it gave me afterwards, but I never enjoyed doing it, so that was always enough to put me off. If I did go for a run, it was usually part of training for some other sport. Why else would I do something I didn't enjoy?

The annual school cross country days were the only other exception. They were the worst days on the primary school calendar, and like most kids, I'd always hope for a well-timed bout of sickness to prevent me from taking part. They were a rare blemish in an otherwise stress-free childhood, and if it were up to me at the time, I would have had them banned and the teachers who organised them sent to court. Looking back, it was almost as if I knew the sport would eventually be my downfall.

With the start of high school came a lot more running and a change in how I approached it. Like everything else in my life, running became an opportunity to put in the hard yards and prove my worth. I didn't see myself as just a kid anymore, so the excuses I used to make no longer held their ground. How much I enjoyed things was losing its relevance, and trying my hardest was fast becoming my default course of action.

With this kind of mindset developing in those first couple of weeks, it's no wonder I was running faster than most of the boys I was racing against. I may have been reasonably fit to start with, but with each run, I pushed myself harder than the one before. All I was doing was trying my best, yet as the days went on, my best got better and better. The bar kept getting raised, and with that, so did the pressure I put on myself to reach it.

One thing very quickly led to another, and before I knew it, what would have been my worst nightmare as a kid became my reality: I was in the school's running team.

***

At first, the coaches said it would involve a few trainings and a day off school. The regional athletics competition was coming up, so the fastest three of us hostel boys were asked to train for the 3km. I may have still hated running, but I was determined to make a good impression at my new school, and skipping a day of lessons to do that seemed like a pretty good deal. Somewhat reluctantly, I agreed to give it a go.

The trainings were just as gruelling as I'd expected, but knowing there were only four of them gave me the mental strength to push through the pain. By the time race day came around two weeks later, I was already feeling the benefits of dedicated training and was fitter and faster than ever before.

In the end, I managed to finish the race in 3rd. My parents decided to come along to watch, and as they watched from the grandstand, they could hardly believe what they were seeing. I'd always been okay at sports, but as far as they knew, running wasn't one of them. It was a great result, and the way I saw it, the perfect way to start and finish a very brief and unenjoyable running career.

From there, I looked forward to focusing on my schoolwork and the sports I was used to – the ones I actually enjoyed. I may have been hungry for success, but I still knew enough about myself to know that running wasn't for me. This made it a no-brainer to turn down the running coaches when they asked me to stay in the team. It was still a notoriously unenjoyable sport, so the way I saw it, no amount of success could justify taking it up full time.

Sadly, the coaches didn't see my situation the same way. I'd already improved so much, so the way they saw it, 'quitting' would be a waste of all my hard work and potential. Besides, the season only lasted a few months, and who knows – I might even start enjoying it.

Ultimately, I agreed to stay on the team because I didn't think I had a choice. The coaches may have had my best interests at heart, but they also made it very clear that my enjoyment wasn't a factor worth considering. I could have just stopped turning up to their trainings, but that's hardly the way to start high school on the right foot. I'd only been there for a few weeks, so if someone with authority told me to do something, I was making damn sure that I did it.

Initially, the coaches told me to just give running a go, but by doing that, I'd already dug myself in too deep. My success-oriented approach to high school was now trapped within a success-oriented sports team. From here, a perfect storm was born.

I had no choice but to run, so the way I saw it, I also had no choice but to run fast.

***

Unfortunately, the next event of the season was a complete success.

It was a relay event, so I raced as part of a team against other schools from throughout the region. The weather conditions were perfect, and we won with a record-breaking time. Of course, it always helps when someone in your team is the fastest in the country, but I was stoked to feel like I played my part, too.

When I went home that weekend, there was another race for me to run. Unlike the others, however, this one had been on the calendar for a while. My older brother, Jack and his mate, Gus, decided to do an endurance race called the Triple Peaks and had asked me a few months back to join their team. Their goal was more about finishing than winning, so this event wasn't one that particularly worried me. I wasn't on their team to help them win. I was just there to make up the numbers.

As the youngest in the team, I drew the short straw of running the first peak, which meant starting with the rest of the pack. It was a 15km leg with plenty of uphill, so although we were in the runners' category, I expected to do a lot of walking. A few freaks always ran the whole way, but they were considered mountain goats amongst men. I certainly wasn't planning to keep up with them.

It wasn't until I started making my way up the hill that I realised walking wouldn't be necessary. Each step felt just as easy as the last, and even when I thought they should be, my legs didn't seem to tire. It was like running in someone else's body. My mind was just being taken along for the ride.

Before I knew it, it was just the mountain goats and me, and after hurtling down the other side of the hill, my job was done, and Jack's began. Having signed up to the event for fun, Jack wasn't too impressed to find himself trying to keep up with that kind of company. Looking back, it was a bit of an unintentional dick-move on my part.

In the end, our team won its category, but all the congratulations seemed to be directed at me. I was the designated star of the show that day, and all of my family and friends were letting me know it. It wasn't often I did well in something my brothers hadn't done well in before, so getting that kind of praise was a weirdly exhilarating experience.

Before then, I'd considered my brothers and me to be one and the same. We'd always been the same size at the same age and had always been good at the same things. I followed in Jack's footsteps, and in due course, my younger brother, Oscar, followed in mine. I guess I'd just assumed this pattern would continue.

Now that I was hearing how fast I was running, I began differentiating myself from my brothers for the first time. If before we'd all been following the same path, now I seemed to be finding my own, and this gave me a sense of identity I'd never had before.

I hadn't necessarily been looking, but it felt at the time like I'd found my niche, and at such a pivotal stage of my development, I latched onto the identity it gave me with both hands. I may not have enjoyed running, but I certainly enjoyed being good at it, so from this point on, I saw it as a big part of the man I was becoming.

With this adjusted identity came adjusted measures of progress and, unfortunately, adjusted levels of pressure to perform. I'd started high school determined to find success, and running had now revealed itself as my way to get there. If before I was having a go at a new sport, now I was competing in something inextricably linked to my self-worth.

I may have started the season well, but I was determined to finish it even better.

***

When you think of a middle-distance runner, what kind of body comes to mind? If you're like me, you're probably thinking of one of those lean, mean African running machines that don't seem to have an ounce of fat on them. One look at the Olympic 5000m line-up and this stereotype can be confirmed.

I still lacked the African skin tone, but the longer I stayed in the running team, the closer I got to that type of physique. That's just what happens when you start growing taller and exercising more without increasing how much you eat. It's not that I was trying to slim down – I just didn't realise how much I needed to eat to avoid it. Besides, there was only so much food I could wolf down at hostel mealtimes, especially as a Year Nine.

As the youngest at my breakfast and dinner tables, I had the job of stacking everyone else's dishes and taking them to the kitchen to be cleaned. Until I did this, the older boys couldn't be released back to their dorms, so ideally, I had to finish my meal before anyone else finished theirs.

I'd like to think I ate my food at an average pace before boarding school, but I soon learned that teenage boys don't muck around when it comes to getting their food down. In that kind of environment, chewing becomes an unnecessary waste of time.

I did have to make some changes to my eating technique, but I was still eating just as much, if not more, at the hostel as I was at home during the weekends. The hostel food was usually pretty good, and if it wasn't, Mum's endless baking and muesli bar supply was there to ensure I never went without.

In the end, though, it just can't have been enough. Without intention or realisation, I began losing weight for the first time.

***

I wasn't necessarily big as a kid, but I had a solid frame and always had plenty of meat on my bones. In fact, up until high school, I played in the front-row of almost every rugby team I'd been a part of.

Like most boys in New Zealand, I'd always dreamed of growing up and playing for the national rugby team, the All Blacks. I was probably unique in my desire to make it as a front-rower, however. It certainly isn't the most glamorous of positions, and the typically plump bodies of front-rowers don't exactly scream peak performance.

As I got further into 2013 and my body continued changing shape, I realised not only that my front rower's dream was getting out of reach but that I no longer wanted it. Each day, I'd hear more comments about how lean and 'shredded' I was looking. Any baby fat I had left was disappearing, and as it did, muscles and bones I didn't know I had revealed themselves for the first time. I was initially indifferent to these comments, but with time, I started relying on them to prop up my self-esteem.

Realistically, I was just losing an unhealthy amount of weight, but I interpreted all the changes I was experiencing as evidence that I was getting better at running. Given what I'd come to believe about success and how it's achieved, it was inconceivable to me that running training was resulting in anything but improvements. In my mind, hard work and sacrifice had become synonymous with success, and with all the effort I was putting in, I certainly felt deserving of some extra perks. If one of these perks was a leaner appearance, I assumed that getting skinnier was what made me faster.

At this point, I began associating how skinny I was with how fast I was running, and before I knew it, the two measures were inextricably linked within my mind. Just as my interpretation of success became linked with sacrifice and hard work a few months earlier, getting skinnier was now my primary measure of progress towards that success. The skinnier I could get, the faster I could run, and the more successful (and eventually happy) I could be.

It was the most dangerous line of thought I've ever had.

***

It's well known these days what foods you should avoid if you want to lose weight. For me, the foods that always stood out were those with lots of carbs. I knew they had a bad reputation in the dieting world, and eating less of them seemed like a pretty easy adjustment for me to make.

Initially, I just stopped eating puddings. We were lucky in the hostel to have each dinner accompanied by something sweet, but I found it reasonably easy to start going without. If any of the boys asked why I wasn't eating them, I'd tell them I didn't have a sweet tooth, and if that didn't work, I'd just have a few mouthfuls before adding it to the rest of my table's scraps. If it meant getting skinnier and better at running, I was more than happy to make the sacrifice.

Unfortunately, this development couldn't have come at a worse time. Term One was drawing to a close, and that meant it was time to start playing rugby. A lot had changed in my life since the previous season, but signing up for a team was still a no-brainer. Running may have become my main focus, but I wasn't going to let that get in the way of the sport I loved most.

As you can probably guess, adding two rugby trainings and a game to my weekly schedule was the last thing my body needed. To make matters worse, the running coaches were now preparing me for cross country Nationals: the final and most important race of the season. It shouldn't have been possible, but having this end date in mind made me start training with even more intensity and purpose than before.

The countdown to Nationals was on, and I wasn't easing off until it was over.

***

With rugby season in full swing and energy-rich foods continuing to be avoided, the demands on my body had never been higher.

My muscles were starting to shrink, and with them went all the strength allowing me to run fast in the first place. There just wasn't as much fuel in the tank as there used to be, and although it was a gradual process, I soon became overtly aware that I was slowing down.

Rugby, too, had become a battle of attrition. You get told as a kid that sports are more fun when you're fit, but any stamina I possessed was now well past the point of offering an advantage. I continued putting every ounce of effort into every training and game I played, but eventually, even that didn't feel like enough. I was half the player I was the year before, and although I was in the lightest weight grade, I could tell that I was playing like crap.

If I'd been thinking rationally, I'd have realised what my body was trying to tell me. I'd have had the awareness to either eat more, exercise less, or, ideally, do both. Unfortunately, the rational part of my brain now had much less of a say than it needed to. My body was screaming at me to make a change, yet my mind was growing increasingly incapable of listening. One fatigue-filled week rolled into the next, and the longer I tried to fight it, the weaker my body and the more irrational my mind became.

The way I saw it, I was slowing down for psychological reasons, not physical ones. The problem wasn't that my body was low on energy, but that I was no longer pushing myself hard enough. I convinced myself the pain and exhaustion were no different from what I'd felt all year, so to get back to my best, I'd just have to toughen up and put up with more of it.

In my mind, pain meant progress, and the closer I got to Nationals, the more obsessed with progress I became. I told myself that if I just kept going until Nationals, then it would all be over, and all the pain and sacrifice would have been worth it. The running could stop, the dieting could stop, and everything that had been so hard about the last few months could stop and never come back. All I had to do was hang in there for another couple of months, and the running season I never wanted would forever be stored away as a success, with the sport never needing to be touched again.

This gave me the mental strength to see the season through, but as you may have guessed, it was yet another link on my growing chain of false beliefs. I may have been rational enough to realise what I was doing to myself was unsustainable, but in no way did I realise how far down the wrong path I'd already travelled. The running season was reaching its end, but my struggles were only just beginning.

I'd already caught the bug, and although I didn't know it yet, the name of that bug was anorexia.

Three

THE SLIPPERY SLOPE

REACHING THE END OF Term One was a relief, but calling the two weeks that followed a holiday is definitely a stretch.

The running coaches, like most people, mistook my weight loss for a more 'shredded' appearance, so they gave me a holiday training schedule on the last day of school. I knew I could get away with ignoring it, but being as obsessively disciplined as I'd become, I followed it to the letter instead. With time targets attached to most runs and rest days few and far between, it was demanding even for the standards I was accustomed to.

Running is an individual sport by nature, but there was always a camaraderie within the team that I really enjoyed. It made me realise I wasn't the only one being consumed by such an unenjoyable sport, and it certainly made trainings less punishing than they could have been.

Going away to compete in events was never too bad, either. The trips were far from my idea of fun, but something about travelling to compete as a team made all the hard work seem worth it. It may have been an unenjoyable sport, but the shared sense of achievement it could generate was something I found pretty inspiring.

To lose the social aspect of running made training over the holidays a completely different kettle of fish. Now that I was training alone, any sense of camaraderie was gone, and the only person I could compare my performances to was myself. When you're only ever putting in your maximum effort, this creates a loop of higher standards and progressively less attainable goals. Each day I had less energy than the day before, yet each day I tried to run faster. It was a battle I was destined to lose from the start.

Lacking teammates to judge my progress against also made my appearance a bigger target for self-scrutiny. Specific features like my face and stomach became checkpoints to determine whether I'd been working hard enough, and with this came a hyperawareness of my body and the way it looked and felt. Any fat I had left was holding on for dear life, yet I was also becoming increasingly aware of its presence. It didn't take long for mirror checks to become my go-to measures of progress, and at that point, getting skinnier shifted from a goal to an obsession.

When you start looking in the mirror several times a day, rarely are there aspects of your appearance that are observably different from before. Aside from superficial features like skin and hair, your biology doesn't operate on that kind of timescale. If there are changes between mirror visits, how 'skinny' you are certainly won't be one of them.

This should have made all those mirror checks seem pointless, but for me, they were anything but. In reality, my reflection may not have changed, but the way I perceived it could vary within hours based on how much I'd been running or what I'd been eating. Deep down, I knew this was irrational, but if there was ever even a hint of uncertainty, I never gave myself the benefit of the doubt. My eyes were seeing one thing, and my mind was seeing another.

In a matter of weeks, I became quick to find fictitious flaws and blind to the deterioration happening right in front of me. What stared back at me was no longer a person but an object to analyse in detail and scrutinise for differences that weren't really there. Under this kind of framework, exercise became my best friend, and it didn't take long for food to become my worst enemy.

***

At one point during the holidays, my family went to Tauranga to stay with friends. There were three kids in their family, too, so we planned to go to the local waterpark one day to kill some time. Waterparks are basically the definition of fun at that age, so this was part of the holiday that I particularly looked forward to.

This made it all a bit confusing when, on the day our parents had arranged to take us, I woke up into what felt like a nightmare. There was a feeling of dread I just couldn't seem to shake, like something terrible was happening, but I couldn't figure out what it was. The world around me appeared to be fine, yet for the way I felt, it may as well have been crashing and burning before my eyes. It was terror like I'd never experienced before, and the worst part was, I didn't have a clue why it was there.

I'd heard the term 'mental health' being thrown around before, but I didn't really understand what it meant until a couple of months earlier. A psychologist came into the hostel one night to help raise awareness, and at one point in his speech, he mentioned mental illness and some key symptoms to look out for.

It shocked me to learn how tough things can get for people inside their heads, and at the time, I remember thinking how insignificant it made my problems seem in comparison. I'd never known anyone with a mental illness, so I felt safe knowing it would never be something that happened to me. I was normal, and from what I could tell, things like 'mental illness' didn't happen to normal people.

So when I woke up that day feeling the way I was, I assumed it was just a case of waking up on the wrong side of the bed. It may have been the worst bad mood I'd ever had, but because I couldn't put my finger on its source, I didn't think I had anything to complain about. Crying in front of everyone was embarrassing enough, so the last thing I wanted to do was share how weird and terrified I felt inside.

Yet the longer into the day my episode continued, the more obvious it became that I was experiencing something much worse than just a bad mood. I'd felt like crap before, as everyone has, but this was a level of crap that I knew must be well beyond normal. I may not have known what it was, but for the first time, I realised that something was wrong with me.

For the past few months, I'd woken up each day determined to find success, and in an attempt to get there, I'd spent part of each day putting my body through the wringer. As the days went by, the standards I set for myself continued to rise as my body's energy stores continued to deplete. Unfortunately, those standards were beginning to exceed what I was physically capable of achieving.

The growing daily demands were coupled with a growing pressure to reach them, and on this particular day, that pressure must have reached its breaking point. What started as a bit of high school motivation had evolved into something terrifying, and to feel the pressure in full force that day must have caught me completely off guard. For the very first time, I woke up to a life I didn't want to live.

After a few hours of bawling my eyes out for reasons I couldn't explain, the other kids eventually lost patience and were taken to the waterpark without me. Dad stayed behind to keep me company, and after waiting in vain for me to pull myself together, he tried getting to the bottom of what was wrong. He asked about everything from girl problems to a fear of waterparks, yet for all his questions, my answer remained the same: 'I don't know why I'm crying.'

The more Dad probed, the more I realised that I didn't have the words to explain what I was feeling and why. All I knew was that something inside my head was seriously wrong, and after finishing the sandwich he made me for lunch, that only one thing in the world would make me feel better – going for a run and, like so many times before, pushing myself as hard as I could.

***

By the time Nationals came around, I was chomping at the bit to wave goodbye and good riddance to the running season I never wanted. It may have only lasted four months, but they were the four worst months I could remember living. Finding myself within hours of it all being over was almost intoxicating.

At the time, I thought being in the running team was the source of all my problems. The way I saw it, that was why life had got so hard and why being me had become such a demanding task. The gruelling runs, the food restrictions, the endless drive to be skinnier – it all seemed to stem back to being part of that team and competing in that notoriously unenjoyable sport. As far as I could tell, finishing the season would make it all go away. It had all started with running, so it would end with it, too.

With this in mind, it's no wonder crossing the finish line at Nationals was one of the best feelings I'd ever had. As with every race and training before, I'd given it every ounce of effort I had, but upon crossing the line that day, I genuinely believed I'd done it for the last time. After accidentally digging myself into a hole a few months earlier, the season was finally over, and at least initially, I seemed to have made it out unscathed.

It was the most challenging period my mind or body had ever been through, yet having made it out the other side, I couldn't have been prouder. I may not have reached the impossibly high standards I set for myself, but having met the coaches' expectations, I finally felt satisfied that I'd done enough. Success is what I'd been searching for, and I knew I'd gone a long way toward finding it.

For the second time that year, I looked forward to returning to a life without running. Focusing on schoolwork had never seemed so appealing, and by only playing the sports I enjoyed, I assumed my route to success was about to get a whole lot smoother. I knew I'd still be motivated to do it all to the highest standard, but with running no longer part of the picture, it was a life that seemed a hell of a lot more liveable than before.

The only problem was, it was a version of life I had forgotten how to live. I didn't realise it yet, but all I'd really done for those past four months was dig myself deeper into a hole, not climb out of one. The season may have been over, but according to anorexia, my work was far from finished.

By that stage, the damage had already been done.

***

Following Nationals, I was back in the hostel with no obligations for the first time in what felt like a long time. Running trainings were a thing of the past, and any rugby trainings I was meant to have that week were cancelled. All I had to do was get through school, and the rest of each day could be spent as I pleased. After such a busy few months, that almost seemed too good to be true.

During my first day back, I just did what any other fourteen-year-old would do – what my mates were doing. We went to the dairy, threw a ball around, watched TV, and generally didn't achieve much. It was an easy way to kill time after school and a small taste of what my post-running season life might look like.

For the first time in months, I felt no different to anyone else. I wasn't a competitive runner anymore – I was just a normal fourteen-year-old spending time with his mates.

Then the guilt started creeping in. At first, it was just the feeling that I was forgetting to do something. After the few months I'd just had, I guess this much could've been expected. Like that weird first day on holiday you get after months of working, I just wasn't used to spending an afternoon the way I wanted. I knew there was nothing I needed to be doing, but the drive that had pushed me forward for so long still lingered like a bad smell.

It wasn't until the next day that this feeling evolved into something more sinister, and at that point, any hope of a more pleasant existence came crashing back down to earth. If the day before I'd felt like I needed to be doing something, now I'd remembered what it was, and to do anything else made me feel like I'd committed some kind of crime. Judged against the standards I'd been setting, I guess I had.

Since starting high school, the rules I lived my life by had become stricter than any human's should. Initially, I just turned up to running trainings and made sure I put in my best effort. Then I took puddings off the menu and started paying more attention to my appearance. Eventually, with rugby added to my schedule, anything less than six consecutive days of hard training felt like a week off, and any fat on my body became a symbol of laziness. Yet the stricter these rules and the more disciplined I became, the stronger the pressure I felt to conform to them and the guiltier I felt when I didn't. The season was over, but the standards I'd set had risen far too high to come back down.

It was less than forty-eight hours since Nationals, and I'd only been doing what my mates were doing, yet already, my mind was overwhelmed with guilt. Guilt for not running, guilt for eating puddings, but more than anything, guilt for having fun instead of pushing myself so hard each day like I was used to.

It was a shocking realisation to have, but it suddenly dawned on me how far from normality I'd drifted. I'd been too engrossed by the running season to notice it before, but now it was over, I could finally see things for what they were. I wasn't the person I was a few months earlier, and now there was a gap in my life that was demanding to be filled. The season was over, but the lifestyle it created was there to stay.

If I'd had more awareness at the time, I'd have realised this gap would close if I'd let it. If I'd sat on that guilt long enough, it would have lost its intensity and eventually, the pressure to push my body so hard each day would have disappeared. The gap would close, and at that point, there would be nothing left to fill.

Unfortunately, I didn't have that kind of awareness. Guilt is an invasive feeling at the best of times, but when you know exactly how to make it go away, putting up with it becomes unbearable.

In the end, I made it stop the only way I knew how – by putting on my shoes, going through my stretches, and without any regard for my exhausted limbs, hitting the pavement and running like hell.

Four

RASH DECISIONS

WITH RUNNING SEASON FINISHED, any rationale I had left for pushing myself so hard each day was gone. There wasn't a need for me to run fast anymore, so although it was a baseless belief to start with, I knew I didn't need to keep getting skinnier, either. I may not have been as rational as I used to be, but this much I could understand. By getting skinnier, I certainly wouldn't do myself any favours.

With running season no longer cramping my style, rugby regained its spot as my number one sporting focus. I'd always been average in height, and rugby is a full-contact sport, so I knew that if anything, I needed to put on weight, not lose it. When playing in the lightest weight grade, only so many times can you be dropped on your arse and maintain your dignity.

I also knew my appearance wasn't getting any easier on the eyes. At the start of the year, my hostel mates told me how 'ripped' and 'shredded' I looked each time I got out of the shower, but as the months went by, the words 'skinny' and 'boney' became increasingly common. Part of me got a kick out of this because it reduced the pressure to be skinny I was so used to feeling. Still, I knew these comments weren't intended as compliments. If anything, they were words of warning.

This made it all a bit confusing when, the week after Nationals, I found myself back doing everything I'd hated so much about the past four months. As it turns out, not wanting to be skinny doesn't mean much when you're addicted to the things that made you skinny in the first place.

I knew I shouldn't be doing them, but like a drug addict who needs their fix, I wasn't thinking about the consequences. I realised that going for runs and skipping puddings would only make me skinnier, but anything that took the edge off that guilt seemed like something worth doing. It was no longer about my body and its performance. At this stage, it was all about my mind and making it feel liveable.

Of course, exercising lots and eating little were terrible strategies for all aspects of my health. They made me feel better about myself in the short term, but the longer these behaviours continued, the more extreme they became. The more I did to avoid feeling guilty one day, the higher the bar was raised, so the more I'd have to do to avoid it the next. It was a vicious cycle, and as the days turned into weeks and the weeks to months, that cycle picked up devastating speed.

At this point, all I was doing was fighting to free my mind from guilt. Soon, my body would be fighting to keep me alive.

***

About a month after Nationals, I started noticing that I was always cold. Granted, it was now the middle of winter, but this was the type of cold that didn't go away. Any clothes I owned were now several sizes too big for me, yet no matter how many layers I had on, a consistent full-body chill remained. I was almost constantly shivering, and whenever I went outside, my hands turned purple and numb.

There was skin, and there was bone, but there wasn't much in between to keep me warm. My body was beginning to suffer at the hands of my already suffering mind.

Around this time, a red patch about the size of a postage stamp appeared on my arm. Initially, I didn't think much of it, but then it started multiplying, and that rang a few alarm bells. Within a week, everywhere between my chin and my knees was covered by the same weird red spots, and a pattern of them branched across my ribcage in the shape of a Christmas tree. It was only August, yet my body was already getting into the Christmas spirit.

That was when I decided to show it to Mum.

Beth Averill (Mum)

I'd noticed Harry had lost weight over the last few months but had put it down to his body streamlining with all the running he'd been doing and his body changing shape with puberty. I'd bought him a school uniform to 'grow into', which obviously covered things up for a while but was now starting to hang off him.

Around this time, Harry told me he'd developed a rash across his torso. Lifting his shirt to inspect, I saw that he did indeed have a nasty rash, but what gave the biggest shock was his incredibly concaved stomach and how tightly the skin wrapped over his ribs. It's something you never want to see as a mother. For the first time, I realised the full extent of Harry's weight loss.

In the end, I went to a dermatologist who diagnosed me with Pityriasis Rosea (AKA 'Christmas Tree Rash'), a rare viral infection most commonly found in pregnant women. The doctor insisted that I wasn't pregnant (phew!) and assured me the rash was noncontagious and would be gone within a couple of months.

While this rash was in full bloom, I was selected in the school's Year Nine rugby team for a one-off game in Palmerston North. The selectors picked me at halfback (the position where size matters least), yet how my minuscule rig made the team still baffles me. It's almost comical to think that just a few months earlier, I was dreaming of a career in the All Black's front row.

Only five minutes into the game, the familiar symptoms of fatigue kicked in. It was like running around with concrete boots on. I was dangerously light, yet all of my movements felt slow and heavy, and by the second half, every step seemed to require conscious effort. Then there were my arms, which were so numb and unreactive that I felt like I was passing the ball around with a couple of unthawed steaks.

At one stage during the game, I must have felt about thirty kilos heavier than I was and decided to run the ball straight into the opposition forward pack (the positions where size matters most). They say that fortune favours the brave, but it certainly wasn't the case this time. I got dealt a good old-fashioned hiding, and by the time I finally made it to ground, I was about twenty metres back from where I started.

We won the game in the end, but I doubt I had much to do with it. Mum and her Mum, Gran, made the trip down to watch, and like all good family members, they were quick to tell me how well I'd played. I didn't believe them, of course, but it was only years later that Mum admitted how worried they'd been watching their stick of a child run around with a bunch of seemingly fully-grown 13-year-olds. Leaving the field with all four of my limbs intact that day was nothing short of a miracle.

With my weight dropping as fast as it was, it should have been a good thing this was my last rugby game of the season. Unfortunately, it wasn't a good thing at all.

***

This time around, I was under no illusion that having more time on my hands would make life easier. The extra time may have been mine to use as I pleased, but if the end of running season was anything to go by, it certainly wouldn't feel that way.

Since leaving the running team a few months earlier, I'd been going for runs whenever I didn't have rugby training after school. I'd then stumble through a rugby game each Saturday before going for a long run from home each Sunday. With rugby season over, I knew I'd have to find new ways to get that pressure and guilt out of my system.

Initially, I replaced rugby trainings with more rugby by playing it socially with mates at the hostel. There was always at least one game happening at that time of the year, so this was a reliable way for me to burn off energy before dinner.

For the other boys, those games would have been another chance to muck around and have some fun after school. For me, they were another chance to put my body through the wringer. There may have been a rugby ball and other players involved, but I wasn't there to play rugby – I was there to exercise. All the rugby did was set a direction for me to run in.

For as long as the games lasted, I ran around trying to cover as much ground as possible and rarely let myself stop moving. Boys aren't very observant at that age, so as far as anyone else knew, I was just one of those dickheads who took social sport too seriously.

By dinnertime, I'd have usually worked myself into a state of exhaustion. For a few weeks, this was enough to relieve the pressure and prevent me from having to push my body further. From there, I'd usually feel relaxed enough to have a reasonably sized dinner and sit through an hour and a half of prep before going to bed.

When I went home each weekend, the pressure would still be there but was never quite as intense. I didn't have to spend half the day sitting down at a desk, so there wasn't the need to cram my exercise into a two-hour timeslot like there was during the week. I'd spend most weekends moving around on my feet, and after adding on a run and a few hundred push-ups, I usually felt like my exercise tally had reached the mark it needed to.

This may seem like a pretty grim weekly schedule, but it did a reasonable job of holding off that guilt, and for long as it did that, I considered it a schedule worth following. As was the case all year, however, the guilt eventually found a way through and with that, the bar was raised higher.

There are only so many hours in a day, and of those I didn't spend in a classroom or dining hall, I was already filling them with exercise. It's no surprise, then, that my diet was what next became vulnerable to manipulation. I guess this was my way of holding off the inevitable pressure to exercise more than I was.

When I woke up each morning, it was like the exercise slate from the day before had been wiped clean, so there was pressure to do just as much exercise, if not more, all over again. By eating less than I had the day before, I realised I could take some of that pressure off. That way, if I didn't reach the ridiculous exercise standards I'd set, the resulting guilt wouldn't be as bad.

Unfortunately, it wasn't just high-carb foods I restricted this time – it was all of them. This was a dramatic shift even for my standards, and not even fruits and vegetables were safe from the cull. High-carb foods made me feel more pressure to exercise than the rest, but it didn't take long for food in general to become the enemy. To eat food was to add pressure to exercise, so the less I could get away with eating, the better I'd allow myself to feel.

Yet the longer I maintained such strictness in my diet, the worse I felt when I did eat food. All I'd tried to do was reduce the pressure I felt to exercise, but in the process, all I'd done was attach it to every crumb that entered my mouth. You know things are getting tough when eating an apple is the highlight of your day, yet even that makes you feel like you need to go for a run around the block.

Eventually, every waking moment came with a pressure to exercise that eating only intensified, and it didn't take long for me to start turning that extra pressure into action. I was already doing a freakish amount of exercise, but in a few more weeks, that would be *all* I was doing.

Five

THE FIRST SICK DAY

UP UNTIL THIS POINT, being in class was my one chance each day to relax. Sitting at a desk is a big part of being at school, and school is just something every five to sixteen-year-old has to attend. I didn't think I had a choice in the matter, so I hadn't previously felt like I needed to do anything but sit down and do my schoolwork during that time.

Unfortunately, this no longer felt like the case come September. I'd already raised the bar to unchartered heights, yet I remained desperate to relieve what was now an intolerable state of mind. My thoughts were being hammered every minute by a pressure to exercise, and unless I acted on it quickly, a growing guilt took its place. I could only put up with it for so long, and after a few days, I cracked.

I knew it was far from a socially acceptable thing to do, but I was past the point of caring what others thought of me. The more days I let that guilt brew inside my mind, the more desperate I became for its absence. I was out of options and very nearly out of my mind. That was when I started exercising in class.

At first, it was just a few squats at the start of each period. I usually got away with this amongst the chaos of everyone grabbing their textbooks and sitting down at their desks. Yet after a few days, the inevitable pressure to do more exercise returned, so I began standing up whenever my teachers had their backs turned. While standing up, I'd usually pretend to tuck my shirt in or pick something up off the floor. This can't have been great for my focus, but neither was feeling like my head was about to explode.

For the first week or so, no one seemed to notice. I guess they just assumed I had a chronic wedgie of some sort. It wasn't until I turned these in-class exercise routines up a notch that I was understandably on the receiving end of a few raised eyebrows.

Initially, it was just the odd head turn from a classmate, but once I started standing up and down several times each period, whispers of 'what the f*** are you doing?' became a lot more common.

Looking back, I guess I was just lucky to have teachers either completely unaware of what I was doing or too confused to comment.

Eventually, standing up in class became too noticeable, so I was forced to reconsider my strategy. Instead, I started holding squats just above my seat. Not only was this less obvious, but it allowed me to burn more energy for longer. It was problem-solving at its finest, and for the next week or so, it allowed me to get through most of my classes undetected.

It wasn't until I started holding these squats for several minutes at a time that I once again came into trouble. As it turns out, holding a squat for too long makes your legs wobble, and when your legs are like twigs, there's more wobble-room than usual. Add on sitting at a confined desk and someone willing to hold the squat well into the wobble-stage, and you once again have a rather noticeable situation.

I could tell from all the head-turning that my classmates were aware of what I was doing, but after a while, they just watched in silence or whispered amongst themselves. I could see in their eyes that they felt sorry for me, but by that point, they must have realised there was nothing they could say to make me stop.

They looked at a boy they no longer recognised, and the boy looking back saw a world he no longer felt part of. All he wanted was that brief thirty seconds of peace when his legs buckled with exhaustion beneath him. All they saw was a boy who'd completely lost the plot.

***

Somehow or other, I made it through to the last week of that term. Given what a term it had been, that was an achievement in itself, and a testament to just how much pain and embarrassment I was willing to put up with.

Over the weekend, Mum sat me down for a pretty serious mother-son chat. We didn't have many of these, so I knew it must be something important. She told me how worried she was about me and what I was doing to myself. The weight loss was getting extreme, and she'd noticed I was eating less and exercising more each time I came home.

There were lots of tears on her end, and I felt terrible that I'd made her feel so bad, but I must have been too shocked at what I was hearing to cry. She asked me if I'd ever considered that I had anorexia, and when I said no, I truly meant it.

I'd accepted something was seriously wrong with me, but I'd genuinely never considered the possibility that I was anorexic. As far as I knew, anorexia was something only girls could get, and no part of my situation seemed to fit the stereotype I had in mind. From what I understood, anorexics were skinny girls who didn't eat enough because, for some reason, they thought they were fat. I wasn't a girl, I still ate things, and I knew that I was far from fat.

It wasn't until Mum told me boys could get anorexia too that I started taking her suggestion seriously. I didn't accept that I was anorexic, but I could appreciate she wasn't entirely barking up the wrong tree. My weight was dropping dangerously low, and I knew whatever was happening inside my head was the cause.

When she reluctantly dropped me back at the hostel on the Monday, we made a pact that when I came home for the holidays at the end of that week, I'd do everything I could to get my life back on track. I'd stop exercising so much, I'd eat more food, I'd put the weight back on, and I'd get back to the happy-go-lucky Harry of old. She and Dad would do all they could to support me, and by the time I returned to school two weeks later, everything would be back to normal. That was the plan, anyway.

As it turned out, she had to pick me up from school just two days later.

***

I'm lucky not to remember much from those last two days in the hostel, but there are a few moments I'll never forget. The first of these happened just before bedtime on what turned out to be my last night.

Prep had just finished, and – as had been the case each time I'd been at a desk for the past two weeks – I'd spent most of it holding a squat above my seat. It was far from my idea of a good time, but it beat the guilt of sitting still, so that was enough.

The good news was, I was now only thirty minutes away from being able to rest my legs, shut my eyes, and go to sleep. The bad news was, unless I wanted to go to bed feeling guilty, that meant I had to do another thirty minutes of exercise.

As had become routine when I entered the dorm, I jumped to grab a beam on the ceiling and did as many pull-ups as I could. The beam was wooden and difficult to grip, so in the past month or so, I'd developed some seriously calloused hands to cope. The other boys had come to expect this performance, so by the time I arrived, about a dozen of them were there waiting to cheer me on. I knew they were only taking the piss out of me, but that didn't bother me nearly as much as it should have.

Another way I'd get my exercise in at that time of day was by locking myself in the shower to do wall squats. The showers were full on this particular night, so I knew I'd have to do my exercise in front of others. In the end, I decided to join a group of boys who were shooting a basketball around outside.

After a few minutes of not getting passed the ball, I eventually gave up and started running around aimlessly, pretending I was playing. It probably looked more like I was running shuttles than playing basketball, and after a few minutes, I probably looked more headless chook than human. Thankfully, I was saved by the bedtime bell after about twenty minutes.

The other boys trailed off to the dorm but for some reason, I just couldn't bring myself to follow. It may seem ridiculous, but even though I'd spent the whole day doing some form of exercise, I still didn't feel like I'd earned the right to sleep. My body felt like it could collapse at any moment, yet according to my mind, there was still work for it to do. Desperate for relief from guilt yet too tired to think of an alternative form of exercise, I started jumping frenetically up and down on the spot.

It didn't take long for other boys to look out their windows and notice what was happening. There I was, under the floodlights of the basketball area with no ball or opponents in sight, repeatedly jumping as high as I could with my eyes squeezed shut and tears streaming down my face.

It wasn't until I'd been jumping for about a minute and had been on the receiving end of numerous 'Harry, what the f*** are you doing?' shouts that I finally stopped and walked defeated back to the dorm. Only then – after doing my usual set of pull-ups on entry and making my way to bed – did I feel satisfied that I'd done enough.

Only then did I let my head hit the pillow and drift into another dangerously deep sleep.

***

It seemed like I'd only just closed my eyes when they snapped open to the sound of the morning bell. It was a new day, which meant it was time to do it all over again. Yet again, the slate had been wiped clean, so yet again, the pressure to exercise was back on.

If I wanted to go to bed guilt-free, I knew I'd have to do just as much, if not more, exercise as the day before. It would start when my feet touched the ground, and it wouldn't stop until my head hit the pillow that night. Only then would I experience those brief few minutes of peace. Only then would all the pain and suffering have been worth it.

I'd just woken up, but I already knew that I couldn't endure another day like that again. If I could have gone to school and behaved like everyone else, I would have, but it had been weeks since I felt in control of my behaviour. Who knew what degrading stunt my mind would make me pull next?

I knew there was only so much weird behaviour I could get away with before I started getting teased, and for the past couple of weeks, I'd been flirting with those boundaries. Making a fool of yourself is one thing. Getting the reputation of a fool is another. I could deal with the constant whispers and stares, but in the last few days, some comments had been cutting deep. My self-respect may have reached an all-time low, but I was only willing to be taken the piss out of for so long.

It made me feel like a complete cop-out, but I just knew that another day at school would be a step too far. My desperate attempts to exercise had dished up more awkwardness in a week than most people get in a lifetime, and I knew it would only get worse. I hadn't had a sick day in over two years, but I decided the time had finally come for my next.

Walking to the shower, I was greeted with the usual gasps as other boys caught sight of me without a top. As usual, I just smiled, said gidday and kept walking before they got a chance to comment further. I wasn't embarrassed to look the way I did, I'd just grown sick and tired of trying to justify to others what felt out of my control. If they did get a chance to ask why I was so skinny, I'd just say, 'It's from that rash I had,' in reply. More often than not, that was enough to get them off my case. It was when they kept asking that the words were hard to come by.

After shivering my arse off – at least, what was left of it – for a few minutes while I waited for a shower, I got to work with a wall squat as I washed myself down. It was noticeably more difficult than the day before, and what usually felt like fatigue now felt much more like nausea. It seemed to take every ounce of willpower I had to keep my legs steady and my vision clear, but as usual, I found a way to make it happen.

From there, I rushed back to my locker to get changed before too many others caught sight of me. Once dressed, I'd usually go wherever my mates were to disguise another wall squat. However, on this particular day, I was understandably not feeling very chatty.

That was when I rang Mum and asked if I could get picked up.

Beth Averill (Mum)

In the past few months, I'd been getting increasingly concerned about Harry. He looked almost skeletally thin and had become increasingly withdrawn and moody. I'd discussed my concerns with our GP and had arranged for Harry to see her that Friday.

I must admit, I was hardly surprised when I got his phone call on Wednesday morning. He said he felt 'dizzy' and 'weird' as if he'd completely run out of energy. By the time I picked him up, Harry was clearly very distressed.

The speed at which things deteriorated from this point was terrifying.

While I waited for Mum to arrive, the rest of the boys went to the dining hall for breakfast. That left about twenty minutes where it was just me, my packed bags, and a whole lot of space to move around. I may have felt more exhausted than usual that day, but you can probably guess what happened next. This time it was press-ups.

I was almost delirious by the time Mum picked me up, but with a twenty-minute car ride ahead of me, I was relieved to have earned the right to sit down. The conversation on the way home was full of concern, but there was a hint of optimism there, too. Mum was relieved to have me back under her care, and I was stoked to finally get away from all those judgemental teenage eyes.

It was Wednesday of the last week of term, so we decided I might as well have the rest of the week off school. That would give me two and a half weeks to get my mind and body back where they needed to be for the final term of the year.

I knew the habits I'd formed would be tough to break, but I was also overtly aware that I didn't have a choice. Realising I could no longer be at school had shocked me to the core, and I didn't want to take any more sick days than necessary.

I didn't know what to expect in the days and weeks ahead, but if Mum's discussion with the GP was anything to go by, I knew I wouldn't be allowed to spend them exercising. This was a strange concept to get my head around, and to be honest, I didn't know how to feel about it. Should I feel relieved? Worried? Guilty in advance?

It wasn't until we got home and Mum served me a plate of toast that the reality of my situation hit me like a ton of bricks. At that point, I knew exactly how to feel. If I couldn't spend the rest of that day exercising, I wouldn't be able to eat a thing on that plate.

Upon realising that, all I felt was fear.

Six

DANGEROUS TERRITORY

My visit to the GP the next day was the first time I'd been to the doctor in over three years. I was only ten the last time, so I had good reason to hardly remember her, and she had plenty of reasons to hardly recognise me. It had been a long time between visits, but I don't think any doctor would have predicted how much about me had changed.

The first thing she did was take my height and weight. I'd always been bang on average for both of these measures, so no one was too surprised to see my height tracking alongside the average for boys my age. Then came my weight, which, as you might expect, didn't bring such good news. I may have grown seven inches taller, but my weight was still the same as when I was ten. Most people change shape when they hit puberty, but it doesn't take a genius to realise the shape I'd changed into wasn't a good one.

After answering all of the doctor's questions and describing my last few months to her as best I could, she didn't have to think too hard to give me a diagnosis. All of the required boxes had been ticked and with that, all of Mum's premonitions were confirmed. I was describing the symptoms of anorexia.

I'd known for a while that what I was experiencing wasn't normal, but to have an official label attached to it did bring a weird sense of relief. Ironically, getting diagnosed with a mental illness was almost what it took to reassure me I wasn't going crazy. It confirmed that my life had turned to shit, but at least I could take comfort from the fact that other people's lives had been shitty in similar ways.

Since arriving home the day before, that shit had been hitting all sorts of fans. Breakfast was a complete write-off, and after spending the rest of the day sitting down, I'd only managed a few mouthfuls of lunch and dinner. It hadn't been from a lack of trying, either.

For each meal, I sat there for about an hour trying to think of a way out of the conundrum I found myself in. I'd repeatedly tell myself that nothing terrible would happen if I had another mouthful and that I'd be strong enough to face the inevitable guilt that followed. I even tried to catch myself napping by taking quick mouthfuls before having the chance to think myself out of it. None of it worked, and any food that did enter my mouth was spat out. I knew how much I was letting myself down and how pathetic it must have looked to anyone else, but even eating what I did made me feel guiltier than I thought possible.

Eating food was like swallowing poison, and the only antidote to the guilt it caused was the exercise I was no longer allowed to do. I'd already accepted that I was obsessed with exercise, but it wasn't until this point that I realised how completely dependent on it I'd become. Without it, food had gone from something I strategically restricted to something I felt mandated not to touch.

Unfortunately, eating isn't the type of inconvenience you can avoid. So, to try and make it possible again, I started exercising as much as I could when my family wasn't looking. I knew I had no choice but to start eating, and getting rid of guilt was the only way I saw that happening. If I could just take the edge off that guilt, maybe I'd be able to see things more clearly. Maybe then I'd be able to justify giving my body the fuel it so desperately needed.

It was a terrible strategy, of course, because the more energy I burned, the more energy my body needed. Clearly, any remnants of rationality had long deserted me by this point. My body was deteriorating faster than ever before, and now it was dragging my mind down with it.

The next day, I decided to spend a few hours back on my feet. It was hardly exercise, but in contrast to sitting down all day, it was enough for me to justify putting energy back into my body.

Sure enough, I managed to eat most of what my parents put in front of me that evening. I felt like the guiltiest man on the East Coast afterwards, but that's beside the point – for the first time since coming home, I found a way to get it down.

Then, like clockwork, the bar was raised, and just like that, the reprieve was over. The following day, spending time on my feet no longer felt like enough, so getting food down was just as challenging as two days earlier. From there, standing up for a few hours evolved into pacing around all day, and it didn't take long for jumping to re-enter the picture, too. As had been the case all year, one thing very quickly led to another, and before I knew it, I was filling every gap I could with exercise.

Eventually, I was burning as much energy as I could get away with under the watchful eyes of my parents, yet even then, I could hardly justify eating anything. I'm sure the food they put in front of me was delicious, but to me, it may as well have been cockroach soup. Either way, I'd be eating as little of it as it took for them to let me leave the table and get back to my feet.

Beth Averill (Mum)

By this point, we all knew something was seriously wrong. I could tell Harry was trying really hard to comply but he was now eating next to nothing.

Then there was the exercise. Harry's room was upstairs, and there seemed to be a constant thumping and banging above us while he exercised out of sight. Whenever I checked what he was doing, he would be in the middle of a segment of press-ups, pull-ups, sit-ups, or planks. He rarely allowed himself to sit down and frequently ran, squatted, and jumped around the house. Even watching him was exhausting, and our attempts to stop him were all but useless.

The one consolidation for me was that he seemed to be sleeping soundly. He was probably so exhausted at the end of each day that he didn't have a choice. It was the only reprieve for any of us. We still thought Harry would be able to come to his senses and that everything would return to normal.

Yet again, we underestimated anorexia.

***

After seeing the GP, I was referred to CAFS (Child, Adolescent and Family Services), who operate under the Hawke's Bay District Health Board. This is standard procedure for any kid having mental health difficulties in New Zealand, as CAFS provide a range of practitioners to them and their families at no cost.

It sounds good in theory, but if my experience is anything to go by, it doesn't always work well in practice. Demand for mental health services is notoriously high these days, and in New Zealand, the sector clearly doesn't have the means to cope. In my case, CAFS didn't have time to see me until the end of the following week. Given the rate my health was declining, this left a dangerous situation for my family to deal with alone.

It's hard to know what the outcome would have been if I'd talked to a mental health professional sooner, as it's possible that once I left school, I was already going down too fast to stop. All I know is that a week is a long time when you're having a mental health crisis, and seeing someone at the start of the week would have given me a much better chance of turning things around. If nothing else, it would have made things much less stressful for my family.

My older brother, Jack, had a rugby tournament that week in a small town called Ruatoria up the coast. It was a big deal at the time, so we'd planned a while back to make the trip up to watch. We were initially going to spend the whole week up there, but by getting myself into the state I had, I'd turned that plan to custard. In the end, we decided the change of scene might do me some good, so we just went up for a few days.

Unfortunately, Ruatoria is more than five hours away, and car travel tends to be done sitting down in a seat. We were lucky to stay with family in Gisborne each way to break up the trip, but three hours was still an intolerable amount of time for me to refrain from exercising.

To make things easier, I downloaded some albums onto my MP3 player before we left. I'd always been a big fan of music, and with over ten hours in a car ahead of me, I thought listening to some new stuff might distract me and help pass the time. It was a great idea, but unfortunately, it didn't quite have the desired effect.

Like most of my good intentions that year, anorexia found a way to use them against me.

Less than ten minutes in, I was already feeling guilty for sitting down, and by the half-hour mark, I was holding squats off the seat as I had at school. The music helped pass the time initially, but then I started using the start of each song as a cue to begin the next squat. By the time my legs collapsed onto the seat a couple of minutes later, the next song was often just around the corner.

Have this process repeat itself for all ten hours I spent in a car that trip, and you can probably appreciate why those albums haven't made it onto any of my playlists since. It was the road trip from hell, and those albums were its soundtrack.

Unfortunately, my time out of the car that trip wasn't much better. When we arrived in Ruatoria, Mum handed me a bottle of liquid breakfast for lunch. I knew it was coming, so I'd been psyching myself up for it for the past half-hour. I'd turned the music to max volume, and to feel less guilty going in, I'd been holding squats with even more intensity and duration than before. Still, I was as surprised as anyone with what I did next.

The bottle had barely touched my hand when I lifted it to my mouth and began sculling its contents. About three gulps later, it was empty, and just like that, my stomach was full. As I handed the carton back to Mum, she looked at me like I'd performed some kind of wizardry. After all the time she'd spent trying to make me eat that week, she was probably wondering why I couldn't have pulled a stunt like that earlier. The way she saw it, that was her job done until dinnertime.

For me, however, the job was only just getting started. Getting the food down was one thing. Putting up with the consequences was the reason I usually didn't eat in the first place.

Needless to say, the hours that followed weren't much fun. Jack had a rugby game that afternoon, but I don't think I watched a minute of it. All I remember is doing push-ups and squats in the ground's car park and swearing to myself that I'd never be so stupid again.

***

Getting home from Ruatoria was a relief, but as you've probably come to expect, things only got worse from there. My upcoming appointment at CAFS was the only glimmer of hope we had left, but then it came and went, and we were only left feeling disappointed. Given the condition I was in by that point, I suppose we were naïve to think any of my problems were ones other people could solve.

The first session involved talking to a family therapist, a clinical psychologist, and a dietitian. I'm sure they all tried their best to help me, but it was all just too little, too late. It wasn't that they were saying the wrong things, it was just far too late for me to hear them. They were teaching me how to play checkers, yet the opponent I was dealing with was already playing chess.

No matter what they told me, anorexia's grip over my mind held firm. I knew as well as anyone that I needed to stop moving and start eating to get back to normal. The problem was, nothing they said got me any closer to making that happen. Getting told what needs to be done is one thing. Getting told how to do it is another. I was already too far down the wrong path, and they seemed too preoccupied with asking me how I'd got there to tell me how to turn things around.

Beth Averill (Mum)

I was eagerly awaiting our first appointment at CAFS and was hopeful they could give us some tips to help Harry. Unfortunately, they spent so long delving into our family dynamics it was like they forgot to tell us what to do. Was Harry like this because he was the middle child? Had there been neglect? Had he been bullied?

Harry was always emphatic that none of these factors applied to him, but it was like they needed a singular cause to figure out how to address the problem. As we know now, there was no single cause for Harry's declining health – it was a combination of many thoughts and events bringing him to that point.

We were probably being overly sensitive, but they also made us feel like we'd done something wrong as parents. I'm sure this wasn't their intent, but despite repeatedly saying we were just a normal family, they kept trying to delve deeper into issues that simply didn't exist.

Ultimately, we left the appointment feeling more helpless and no further ahead.

By the second week of the school holidays, it was obvious I'd need a lot more sick days than first thought. Any hope of a quick return to normality had all but vanished. I'd been heading in the wrong direction for a while, but since leaving school, my life had unravelled further and faster than I could have ever imagined.

I felt like a servant to the anorexic part of me, relentlessly striving for the unobtainable standards that it set. I knew my behaviour was only making things worse, but my version of reality was becoming so twisted that I no longer saw an alternative. To do anything other than obey those anorexic thoughts was inconceivable, and to even think about standing up to them was a guilty sin in itself.

Yet the most dangerous thing about anorexia is that the more religiously you adhere to its standards, the more ridiculous they become. Then, once those standards are so absurd that reaching them could literally kill you, your brain is too malnourished, and your mind is too tormented for you to care. Starvation is to anorexia what fuel is to a car, and death is the place it tries to take you. The less energy your brain has left to work with, the more powerful the illness becomes.

By this stage, I was already experiencing starvation's weird and wonderful symptoms. For one, some bizarre things were happening with my hair. The stuff on my head used to be thick and wavy, but just like the person whose head it sat on, what was left of it was now brittle and thin. Then there was the rest of my body, which had a soft, feathery coat of hair called lanugo. I didn't know it then, but as with my purple hands, this was another of my body's attempts to keep my organs warm using what little energy it had left.

Then there was my heart, which was causing my family all sorts of concern. It's common for endurance athletes to have low heart rates, and given how hard I'd pushed myself all year, mine had probably been low for a while. It wasn't until Mum brought a monitor home from work that we realised the dangerous extent it had dropped. Unlike most athletes, mine wasn't a sign of cardiac efficiency but a tired heart that was struggling to keep up.

A consequence of this was how dizzy and lightheaded I felt. I'd been noticing this for a while, but in the past couple of weeks it had become impossible to ignore. Moving from place to place seemed to require my full attention, and my vision often went patchy as if it was about to fade to black.

Fortunately, it never did – my eyes remained open, and my legs remained steady enough to keep me on my feet. Unfortunately, that meant the exercise had to continue.

Beth Averill (Mum)

Harry was now looking gravely ill. He was pale (almost blue in the face) and looked noticeably skinnier each day. Despite this, he continued eating next to nothing and was exercising whenever he could.

I'd been reading everything I could about anorexia, so I knew we needed to be keeping an eye on his heart. When I brought a heart rate monitor home from work, I was shocked to see how low it was and even more shocked to see how much it dropped the following day.

I rang the GP, who told us to prepare for hospital admission.

When my second session at CAFS came and went with as little success as the first, we knew things were about to get a lot more serious. There was clearly nothing anyone could do to change my behaviour, and I was already well beyond the point of being able to initiate that change myself. My decline was inevitably set to continue, and I knew as well as anyone that I didn't have much room left to fall.

Death was the only plan anorexia had for me, and the more days that went by, the closer it got to achieving its goal. One week rolled into the next, and as anorexia continued dragging me down its dangerous path, all my mind could do was surrender, and all my body could do was hang on for dear life.

From this point, things could have gone one of two ways: either I went to hospital, or my body gave up on me before I had the chance. Neither were particularly appealing options, but if one thing was for sure, things couldn't continue the way they were. Something, soon, would have to give.

As grim of a predicament as this may seem, there was something about it that I found oddly reassuring. Whatever path my life took next – be that hospital or one with a dead end – I'd soon lose the responsibility of keeping my body alive. In one case, the responsibility would pass into the much more capable hands of doctors and nurses. In the other, it would cease altogether. As far as I could tell, this meant that whatever came next, anorexia would no longer be the one deciding my fate. It could only drag me down so far because there was only so much of one life it could ruin.

In my eyes, the sooner I reached that crossroads, the better.

I give up

I'm done

you finally have won.

I surrender

to your pleasure

to your goals that do not measure.

10/2013

Seven

HITTING ROCK BOTTOM

IT WAS MONDAY 14TH of October 2013, the first day of the new school term, my fourth consecutive sick day, and, as it turned out, the worst day of my entire life.

It was a tough day for all sorts of reasons. The only words I spoke were a few murmurs to my parents, the only food I ate was a grape at breakfast, and all I did aside from that was exercise. I continued covering as much distance with as many hops, skips and jumps as my body could manage, and I did it all with a grimace on my face. However, the real kicker was what happened that evening.

As had become routine, Mum was sitting on the edge of my bed, waiting for me to drop off to sleep. Any moment I was alone and conscious was a moment I tried to exercise, so to have her there was reassuring for us both. Like every other night, she'd just spent a few minutes telling me everything would turn out okay and that tomorrow would be a better day. I'm not sure if she believed it, and I certainly didn't, but it was comforting all the same. I'd have usually dropped off to sleep by the time she finished speaking, but tonight was different. Tonight, instead of sleeping, I was crying.

I'm not ashamed to say I'd cried a lot that week, but this was more than just a cry – it was a complete breakdown. I'd lived in what felt like a nightmare for months, but the terror I felt at that moment was unlike anything my brain had ever conjured up before.

More than anything else, I felt trapped inside a mind that was no longer mine. It was like my consciousness was suffocating with no room to move, surrounded at all angles by heavy pressure that impinged every thought. With no means of escape, all I could do was exist and be hammered by anorexia's merciless darkness.

We don't usually think of mental pain as excruciating, but maybe we should, because whatever I felt that night must have come close.

In the end, gritting my teeth, grimacing, and groaning through the internal onslaught no longer felt like enough. All I wanted to do was escape from those feelings, yet the more I struggled, the more trapped in that terrifying loop my thoughts became. In the end, I tried to escape the pain the only way I knew how – by running away from it.

Like a boy possessed, I leapt out of bed and ran out of my room. I didn't know where I was going – all I knew was that I needed to run. After hurtling down the stairs three at a time, I then made a frantic bolt for the front door. It was the only thing left between me and the expansive night beyond – the only obstacle left in my desperate dash for freedom.

What I didn't realise was that Mum – a handy sprinter in her high school heyday – was hot on my heels, and just as I was breaking clear of the door, she slammed it shut behind me. Ninety-nine percent of me made it through, but like a mouse getting the tip of its tail caught in a trap, one percent of me didn't. The longest finger of my trailing hand was the only part of me caught, but it was enough to bring my escape attempt to a very abrupt stop.

My parents always told my brothers and me that if you're going to do a job, you might as well do it well. Well, Mum practised what she preached on this occasion because she sure did an excellent job of that finger. My heart wasn't beating as fast as it should have been, but the blood going to that hand certainly didn't seem in short supply. It was pouring out like it had somewhere else it needed to be.

Dad had joined the party by this stage, and between him and Mum, they soon had me huddled up with them on the sofa. I'd lost quite a bit of blood by this point, but after wrapping my finger in tea towels and applying some pressure, they were able to bring the bleeding to a stop. That should have put an end to all the drama, but it didn't. At that point, my entire body started shaking.

I'm not sure what caused this, but I know that mentally and physically, it was about the worst I'd ever felt. Mentally, I felt like I wanted to die, and physically, I felt like I was about to. I was like a kid getting helped out of a nightmare by his parents, only this nightmare wasn't one they could wake me up from. Eventually, they carried me like a baby back up to my bed, and after shaking uncontrollably for a about an hour, I dropped off to sleep in their arms.

Beth Averill (Mum)

I remember that night like it was yesterday. I'd been trying to convince Harry to let himself go to sleep yet noticed he seemed even more agitated than usual. Then, out of nowhere, he made a run for the door.

His mangled finger was not a pretty sight, and I felt so bad to have caused it. Harry looked utterly broken. He just shook and whimpered as I tried to stop the bleeding as best I could. I spent the rest of the night lying beside him, checking if he was still alive.

I thought we might lose him that night. As it turned out, we probably almost did.

I've often wondered what would have happened had that door not slammed on my finger. Would I have run off like a madman into the night, refusing to stop until my body did first, or would I have come to my senses and saved my parents the search party? I'd like to think the latter, but the former seems much more likely given the circumstances.

Yet as terrible as that night was, getting my finger slammed in that door was probably the best luck I'd had all year. Not only did it stop me from running off perilously into the night, but it also won me the help I desperately needed.

The next day, Mum took me to get my finger dealt to by a nurse. It was grim to look at, but luckily, she told us it wasn't anything too serious. While we were in the medical practice, Mum asked on the off chance whether my GP was free for a chat. She was reaching her wits-end with worry and was desperate for a professional to tell her what needed to be done. My next CAFS appointment was still a few days away, and she knew I wouldn't make it that far.

As luck would have it, my GP was available, and a few minutes later, she had me lying on a bed to check my heart. The time between visits was only three weeks this time instead of three years, but the change wasn't any less dramatic.

Not only did I look awful, but my heart rate and blood pressure told her I was well within the range of something called bradycardia. Anorexia has the highest mortality rate of any mental illness, and medical complications such as this account for over half of all deaths. What was a serious concern three weeks ago had turned into something life-threatening, and to prevent me from becoming another statistic, my GP knew she needed to be the one to act.

The following morning, less than three weeks after being diagnosed with anorexia, I was admitted to hospital.

Eight

TWO SIDES OF THE SAME COIN

THE HOSPITAL STAFF PUT me in a sunny room with a big window and a blossom tree outside. There was a restroom near the entrance, a TV on the wall and some visitors' chairs in the corner. It wasn't anything special, and I couldn't have cared less about the aesthetics, but as far as hospital rooms go, it was a score.

When I first arrived, it took a while for any hospital staff to check on me, so I spent a few hours burning off what little energy I had left. Mum was in there with me, but she eventually gave up trying to make me stop. If there was one thing she'd learned in the past few weeks, it was that when it came to my behaviour, anorexia had much more of a say than her.

When a doctor finally arrived, he was understandably unimpressed with what he saw. Here was a boy – or at least, the remnants of one – who was meant to be on 24/7 bed rest yet was jumping around his hospital room like it was some kind of gym. I don't imagine it was the type of situation he was used to.

Thankfully, he immediately realised the danger of my situation and was able to convince me to get off my feet and onto the bed. Then, after asking lots of questions, checking my heart, and attaching a cardiac monitor to my chest, he told me what would be happening going forward.

He started by saying that I'd be on bed rest around the clock. I knew this was inevitable, but given the life I'd been living for the past few months, it was still a tough pill for me to swallow. Rarely in the past few weeks had I been awake and not on my feet, so the prospect of staying in bed every hour of the day was almost inconceivable. Luckily, he also convinced me I didn't have a choice.

Then he brought up food. It was too dangerous for me to go another day without it, so tonight, I would start getting fed the nutrients I desperately needed. In a couple of hours, a nurse would arrive to help me get down dinner, and it would be in my best interests to do all that I could to finish it. If I didn't, a tube would be put up my nose and I would be fed through that instead. Either way, the food would find its way to my stomach, so whether I liked it or not, the fast would have to end.

I listened intently to everything he said, and as much as it made me dread the days ahead, it also gave me hope. My life could have gone one of two ways, and as appealing as the alternative had seemed, I felt grateful it went the way that kept me alive. No one would let me die now that I was in hospital, so the way I saw it, getting better was the only way forward. If I had no choice but to stop exercising and start getting fed, then from what I could tell, anorexia would be stripped of all its power. Those were the only tools it had in its toolbox, and now they'd been taken away, I assumed the illness would finally bugger off and leave me alone.

I assumed wrong.

***

A nurse came in with my food tray at around five o'clock that evening. On the menu that night was mince, mashed potato, and peas; nothing special, but nothing to complain about, either. It was a good hearty feed for a boy who needed about a hundred.

Luckily, the nurse on duty was an absolute legend with lots of experience dealing with anorexic patients. She put the food tray in front of me, sat beside my bed, and said all the right things as I attempted to get through my first proper meal in over two weeks. Any words she spoke were encouraging, and it helped to know she understood how difficult each mouthful was for me. When you're trying to eat what your mind is screaming at you not to touch, empathetic support like this is vital.

After eating so little for so long, the entire process seemed foreign. The food's texture felt weird in my mouth, and I was hyperaware of its presence as it stretched its way down into my tiny stomach. These sensations only made things more difficult, but thankfully, I still found a way to get the job done. About an hour after that first mouthful, my plate was empty, and my first meal in hospital was officially a success.

The nurse was quick to shower me with praise and let me know that the significance of the achievement wasn't lost on her. She told me I'd just finished the hardest meal of my life and assured me eating would only get easier from there. I believed her, and as strange as it was to get praise for something I felt so guilty about, I was proud to have made what felt like my first step of my recovery.

With the support of my family now combined with that from the hospital staff, I felt for the first time like I had the strength to rival anorexia. A return to normality no longer seemed so far beyond my reach, and the nightmare I'd lived in for so long didn't seem quite as dark as before. There was a long way to go, but at least I'd finally made a start.

***

I woke up that night to the sound of hurried footsteps and panicked medical chatter. Half a dozen people dressed in scrubs were standing over me, frantically checking my cardiac monitor and asking if I felt okay.

When I told them I felt fine, I meant it. Granted, I felt a bit tired, but so would most people at one in the morning. The doctors and nurses didn't seem to believe my response, so after watching them stare at me like I was an alien for another few minutes, I eventually drifted off back to sleep.

It wasn't until the following day that I realised how lucky I was to have made it through the night. Since being attached to the monitor the day before, my heart was beating well less than once a second, and at times during the night, it was beating less than once every two. My medical knowledge was pretty limited at this point, but even I could understand that thirty beats a minute wasn't ideal. The heart shouldn't have to conserve energy, and if it's conserving as much as that, it's probably been struggling for a while.

I'd felt like my body was about to give up for the past few weeks, but to realise just how close it came was still a shock. The doctors told me that if I'd gone another day without food, the outcome could well have been different. Another day living life the way I was, and the heart that was already so tired may have stopped beating altogether. Another day living life on anorexia's terms, and this story could have ended right here.

It's a scary thought, and to think how many variables could have played out differently in the few days prior only makes it scarier. Thankfully, only one thing mattered: I was still alive, and that meant anorexia hadn't won yet.

***

My physical health was what kept the doctors concerned, but my mental health was what made me feel so rough the next morning. Once awake, I'd usually be straight onto my feet to get rid of any early morning guilt. Now that I was in hospital, being on my feet wasn't an option. I was under strict instructions to stay in bed, or in other words, to let that guilt brew from the get-go. To my body, it was heaven. To my mind, it was hell.

You'd think getting told I'd almost died the night before would be enough to make me start going easier on myself. My body clearly needed the rest, and my mind clearly needed to break free from the habits that put me where I was. Yet after spending the past fifteen hours on bed rest, my motivation to stay alive didn't even come close to my motivation to feel less guilty. I knew it was in my long-term interests to just lie down and relax, but all I could focus on was getting that short-term peace of mind.

Fortunately, as strong as my impulses were to jump out the window and make a run for it down the main street, I convinced myself that getting out of bed wasn't an option. It may not seem like it, but a big part of me still wanted to avoid getting into trouble. Getting told off by my parents was one thing, but getting told off by doctors and nurses felt like a step too far. As obedient as I'd become to the illness inside, there were still some voices on the outside that had enough authority to influence my behaviour.

In the end, I guess I made a compromise between the internal and external noise. I could accept I had to stay in bed, but there was no way I was going to sit there passively. All I wanted was to feel better about myself, and if I couldn't do that through exercise, I could at least try to mimic the experience. Desperate times call for desperate measures, and when it comes to anorexia, bizarre behaviour.

Without thinking about what I was doing, I started tensing my entire body as hard as I could. I held the tense until my muscles screamed at me to stop, and only then did I let myself relax back onto the bed. Just like the exercise I was used to, there was a shortness of breath and a pain in my muscles, but more importantly, the same wave of guilt-free relief that washed over me when I stopped. It may have only lasted a few moments, but in those blessed moments, my mind finally felt at peace. Then the guilt of not exercising returned, so I jammed my body back into a tense and started again.

This may seem like a very calculated way of getting around my exercise cravings, but I was really just acting on impulse. Only after years of reflection have I made sense of it all and figured out why I felt the need to behave so strangely.

As it turns out, I wasn't addicted to exercise but to the pain and exhaustion I was so used to accompanying it. Continually pushing through those feelings and finding myself on the other side of them is ultimately what gave me the peace and satisfaction I craved. In my mind, pain meant progress, so whenever I wasn't putting my body under some kind of stress, I felt guilty.

It all comes back to that mindset I developed earlier in the year. Desperate to grow up and be successful, I arrived at high school determined to work as hard as I could. Then I found myself in the running team, and from there, I started directing all that hard work into running faster.

Yet as the year went on and anorexia started taking hold, the standards I set for myself kept rising to dangerous heights. Eventually, maintaining those standards was nothing about getting better at running and everything about avoiding the guilt of not working hard enough.

Yet the longer this continued, the stronger that guilt became and the greater the lengths I had to go to get rid of it. In the past couple of months, it had been there every minute of every day, and as I was finding out now, pushing myself to the brink of death still wasn't enough to make it go away. I wasn't allowed to exercise anymore, but according to anorexia, I still had to put my body through some kind of pain.

The hospital staff didn't understand what I was doing or why, but judging by the grimace on my face every few minutes, they could tell I wasn't resting like I was supposed to. Their attempts to stop me from tensing were all but useless, and as the day went on, the less obedient I became to them and the more obedient I became to anorexia. They couldn't stop me because I'd lost the ability to stop myself.

Beth Averill (Mum)

Having Harry admitted to hospital was a huge relief. We'd been on 24/7 watch for the past few weeks, so it was reassuring to know he was finally safe and getting the care he needed.

Aside from supervised trips to the toilet and shower, Harry wasn't allowed to leave his bed. I knew how hard this would be for him, so I asked the staff if he could go for the odd walk down the corridor. They insisted Harry needed to conserve as much energy as possible, so there could be no bending of the rules. As a result of this, Harry found a way around them.

I found his tensing ritual so distressing to watch – it was a constant reminder of how tormented he was inside.

***

Eating dinner the night before got my hospital stay off to a positive start, but I soon realised that my nightmare was far from over.

With my mind already so full of guilt, the last thing I wanted was to add to it by eating breakfast. Eating had become something I had to work for, and after the laziest fifteen hours of my last five months, I felt nowhere near deserving of that experience.

On the flip side of being addicted to pain, I'd essentially become allergic to experiencing pleasure. For the same reason putting myself through pain relieved me from guilt, experiencing pleasure seemed to make it worse. Pain felt like progress, and pleasure felt like intemperance. They were two sides of the same anorexic coin, and because a lot of what we find pleasurable keeps us alive and makes our lives worth living, this side of the coin was no less brutal.

It's a common misconception, but just because I was anorexic doesn't mean I didn't enjoy food. If anything, I was so deprived of it that it tasted even better. Like drinking when you're thirsty or going to the toilet when you're busting, eating when you're hungry is one of life's greatest pleasures.

The only aspect I didn't enjoy was how guilty it made me feel. Before hospital, most of that guilt came about because I was putting energy into my body. The more I ate, the more pressure I felt to burn it off, so the guiltier it made me feel and the less inclined I was to eat in the first place.

Now that I was in hospital, that type of guilt no longer held its ground. I knew that if I didn't eat the food myself, the nurses would feed it to me through a tube instead. This stripped me of responsibility for taking that energy on. After all, it wasn't my fault it was entering my body, but the doctors' and nurses' keeping me alive.

This should have made eating food seem easier now that I was in hospital, and it did, but on that particular morning, it still wasn't enough to make eating breakfast possible. Food tasted good, and for that reason alone, my brain told me I wasn't allowed to eat it. I knew it was irrational, and I hated feeling like I was letting everybody down but unfortunately, I didn't even feel close to making it happen.

It seemed like they'd just taken my breakfast tray away when they replaced it with a lunch tray, and when that too was left untouched, the hospital staff had to take matters into their own hands. Just as promised, a tube was inserted up my nose, down my throat, and into my alarmingly empty stomach.

For the rest of that day, the nurses fed me a high-energy nutritional supplement (Fortisip) through the tube in my nose, and I had no choice but to sit in bed and feel my stomach grow full. The calories went in, my body's energy stores continued to replenish, and through that slow form of mental torture, I lived to see another day.

Nine

FOUR WHITE WALLS

I WAS VISITED BY my CAFS team the following day. Thankfully, my team now included a psychiatrist who seemed to really know his stuff. He asked plenty of questions and furiously jotted every answer down into his old-school notebook.

I got the feeling he found me to be an intriguing case. I'd let anorexia take my exercise and eating habits to such unhealthy extremes, yet at the same time, I seemed precisely aware of how irrational it was. I was determined to get back to normal, yet at the same time, I remained blindly obedient to the illness barking orders at me inside my head.

What also made things interesting was how many of anorexia's friends and family had joined the party. Depression, OCD, anxiety, and even psychosis were there playing a part in the craziness. All were contributing their time and talents to the melting pot of mental illness my life had become.

After talking to me for about an hour, the psychiatrist brought up medication. There were three drugs he suggested I start taking, with each designed to target a different aspect of my illness. Provided I responded well to them over the next few weeks, the intention would be to increase the dose of these drugs going forward.

I didn't know the first thing about neuropharmacology but decided if there was even the slightest chance those drugs could help, taking them would be a good idea. The decision to take medication always needs to be made from a personal context, but it was a no-brainer for my family and me. The drugs were tried and trusted, and even if they hadn't been, it seemed unlikely they'd make things any worse for me than they already were.

Also visiting me that day was the dietitian. The objective of the hospital staff was to make me put on weight as fast as possible, so her job was to decide the maximum amount of food my malnourished body could safely take on. She was lovely, and we got on well, but thanks to her job description, the anorexic part of me hated her with a passion.

Ever since getting the tube put in the day before, I'd watched with horror as the Fortisip flowed down from a stand into my body. As soon as one bottle emptied, a nurse came in to replace it with another. I wasn't used to having so much food on board, and I felt almost consistently bloated, or the way I interpreted it, fat.

Whenever I looked to my right and saw the bottle of what would soon be in my stomach, I felt a dread so intense that it may as well have been filled with poison. Then, almost like clockwork, I'd start tensing my entire body as if compensating for the fact I was going to put on weight.

The hospital staff eventually caught wind of this, so to make the weight-gaining process more manageable, they started hiding the bottle behind a curtain. This certainly made things easier, but I still felt the almost constant chill of the tube as it carried Fortisip down the back of my throat.

What made things worse was that whenever breakfast, lunch or dinnertime came around, I had to sit for half an hour with the meals going cold on my lap. They were the caloric equivalent of what eventually went down the tube, so even compared to typical teenage boy standards, each meal was massive. This was unfortunate because, like most anorexics, I'd developed almost savant-like abilities in judging the caloric content of food. I was acutely aware of much energy was going in and, regrettably, just how little I'd be burning off.

The staff assumed that I'd eventually start eating, in which case, less Fortisip would have to go down the tube. I understood their rationale, and staying optimistic is essential, but it should have become clear quite quickly that I wasn't having a bar of those supersized portions. By the time the meals made it onto my lap, the red flags were already up, and any hope of having that first mouthful was already gone. They were an instant reminder that I was putting on weight, so from there, letting myself experience any form of pleasure was out of the question.

From that point, all I wanted to do was put myself through pain.

these walls, they trap me

these four white walls are full of darkness

my mind is a battlefield of thoughts

but I am in my mind

more walls

inside, I am trapped

in my very own

tight black bubble

11/2013

***

My body was finally getting the nutrients it needed to stay alive, but anorexia was nowhere near finished with my mind. It was fighting harder than ever to maintain control, so although it could no longer kill me, it was doing all it could to make my life hell.

The doctors' orders were in direct conflict with what my thoughts told me to do, and as much as I hated being such a pain in the arse, I felt like I had no choice but to act on every compulsion that entered my head. Hardly a minute went by where I didn't hold my body in a tense, and the more meals I left untouched, the less likely that first mouthful became.

The staff eventually decided I needed a 'watcher' in my room at all times. Watchers are officially known as Health Care Assistants, and their job is to provide extra support for patients who need it. In my case, their job description was simple: watch his every move, and if you see him do that weird tensing thing, try to make him stop.

I had a different watcher for each hospital shift and six in total. My family and I got on well with all of them, and as the days went by, they all developed their own techniques to stop me from tensing. One lady tried to distract me by giving me crosswords, one tried to comfort me by giving me hugs, one tried to overpower me with her brute strength, one tried to rationalise with me by talking, one tried to scare me by shouting, and obviously out of options, one just sat there praying. Needless to say, some shifts went by easier than others, and as hard as they all tried, no watchers even came close to keeping me relaxed.

It was tedious for everyone involved, and if I'm being honest, there were times I wished anorexia had just finished me off when it had the chance. Each day was just as bleak as the last, and as my first week in hospital rolled into the next, the nightmare only got scarier. My body's energy stores continued to replenish, yet my mind continued to be punished for it with guilt. It was relentless, and as much as I'd like to say that bed rest got easier with time, it didn't.

The longer I spent in hospital, the more obvious it became that I was putting on weight. I knew it was inevitable, and I knew how important it was for my recovery, but that didn't make it any easier to deal with. As I watched the calories pour into my body, I couldn't help but feel like all the hard work I'd done that year was being undone. I only put on about a kilo in that first week, but for how I felt, that may as well have been ten.

Where skin hugged tightly around my bones, there was now a bit of wriggle room. Where there used to be nothing, now there was something. I'm not sure if I was hyperaware of these changes or if my mind was playing tricks on me again, but it all resulted in the same thing: guilt, guilt, and you guessed it – guilt.

To anyone else, I looked just as freakishly skinny as when I entered hospital a week ago, but to me, I'd already piled on so much weight that I was unrecognisable. Judging against anorexia's standards, I may as well have been obese.

***

My life may seem pretty grim at this point, but it wasn't all bad. Compared to most people with a mental illness, I was well and truly one of the lucky ones.

I may have been the only one experiencing what I was inside my head, but at no point did I feel like I was facing my battles alone. There was enough love and support around me to sink a ship, and no matter how self-centred and irrational my behaviour probably seemed, that love and support never once wavered.

For one, I couldn't have asked for a better family. There isn't a guidebook telling you what to do when someone close to you has a mental illness – all you can do is everything you can. My parents didn't always know what to say to make me feel better, but they spent every moment they could sitting next to my bed. Anything they did say was positive, and I'm not sure if they believed it, but they told me every day that I was strong enough to make it out the other side. Hearing their belief in me was everything – I could only hear it for so long before I started believing in myself.

My younger brother, Oscar, was only ten at the time, but he came and saw me every day once he'd finished school. It didn't matter that he didn't understand what was going on. If anything, it was a bonus because it made him treat me like the same big brother he'd always known. He had a refreshing outlook only kids can have – as far as he knew, I'd be back to my usual self in no time.

My older brother, Jack, may have better understood what was happening, but he was no less optimistic. Each weekend he'd come in, shake my hand, and yarn away to me like nothing was wrong with the world. I'd catch up on all the latest goings-on in the hostel and hear of him and all his mates' latest antics. We never talked about the touchy-feely stuff, but we didn't need to. No matter what happened, I knew he'd always have my back.

Then there were my grandparents, who were about as good as grandparents come. Not a day went by without them in it, and every one of those days was a lot better for it. No grandparent should ever have to visit their sick grandchild in hospital, but mine happened to be pretty damn good at it. They passed on the type of wisdom that can only be gained with age and were the only ones who ever found a way to make me laugh. Unfortunately, the jokes my Papa told aren't ones I can ever repeat.

Only close family were allowed to visit me, so aside from illegal break-ins from my aunty, godfather and dog, the rest of that love and support came in the form of cards. From family and friends across New Zealand to cousins travelling in Canada and Antarctica, colourful bits of paper eventually plastered my walls.

Yet of all the cards I got, my favourite was the monstrosity I got from my mates at the hostel. Each of them wrote a personalised message for me, and as thirteen to fourteen-year-old boys often do, most kept it short and almost offensively to the point. The following are a pretty fair reflection of the rest:

Sup Haz, I hope you get better real soon. We are all missing you in the hostel and in our rugby games. Chur.

Hey Haz, I hope you get better soon because we need you back for cricket.

Hi Hazza, thinking of you bro. Mum has told me everything and it's quite scary but you're strong and can get through this.

Hey Haz, I'm going to beat you next time I race against you. You will be getting slow and unfit in hospital. Sys.

Clearly, some boys had a better grip on my situation than others, but each of these messages meant just as much. If anything, those with slightly the wrong tone were the ones I enjoyed reading the most. For a few moments, they made me forget that anything was wrong with me. I was just one of the boys, and as long as we scored tries in rugby and made runs in cricket, there was nothing we had to worry about.

There was a strength that came with knowing how many people were rooting for my recovery, and thinking about it never failed to inspire me. I may have found myself in an unfortunate set of circumstances, but on the whole, I was still one very lucky kid. As dark as things were inside my head, the world around me never failed to shower me with light. For that, I will always be grateful.

***

By the end of my third week, the hospital staff talked about transferring me to another hospital. My heart was back doing what it should, my weight had been rising steadily, and my body had been topped up with all the vital nutrients it needed. I was still a long way off what they called my 'target weight', but as far as the staff at Hastings Hospital were concerned, their role in my recovery was nearing its end.

The only problem they couldn't fix was my mind, which was still in just as bad a shape as before. The medication wasn't yet having an effect, and as the days went by, my compulsive behaviours became increasingly habitual. I continued tensing up every few minutes, and the meals continued going cold on my lap before getting taken away. Whatever came next on my road to recovery, it clearly couldn't be a return home.

Instead, they decided to transfer me to the adolescent psychiatric ward of a hospital just out of Wellington. It's known as the Rangatahi Unit, and I'd be joining around fifteen other patients there from across the North Island. The staff at Hastings Hospital had done all they could to bring me back to health, but without the ability to improve my state of mind, there wasn't any more they could do. A psych ward was now the best place for me. Once there, I'd have everything I needed to get my life back on track.

Naturally, my family was gutted. The Unit was almost four hours away, so they knew I'd be spending most of my time down there without them. Mum and Dad pleaded with me to find a way to turn things around and prove to the doctors they could send me home, but deep down, I think they knew the right call had been made. Being transferred to another hospital may have seemed like a step back, but sometimes a step back is what's needed to find a new way forward.

Unlike my family, I was indifferent to the idea. It was a bit like the decision to start taking medication. As far as I could tell, things couldn't get worse than they already were, so if being in a psych ward was what the doctors thought was best, that was where I'd go. I knew I wasn't making any progress where I was, so the way I saw it, any change of scene would be better than none. Anything would be better than staying between those four white (now very colourful) walls.

***

My fourth and final week in Hastings Hospital went by much like the ones that had gone before: in short, terribly. Unlike the others, however, this one did offer slight glimmers of hope.

Now that I'd put on a few kilos, the doctors allowed me to have a supervised walk down the corridor each day. They only lasted a few minutes and weren't allowed to be more than a stroll, but after weeks of being confined to a bed, even that made a difference to my state of mind. It was a drop in the ocean of what I put my body through a month earlier, but a guilt-reliever all the same.

Something else that changed that week were my mealtime arrangements. Instead of bringing in the supersized food portions I was meant to eat, the nurses agreed to just serve me a few mouthfuls and put the rest of the calories down the tube. This spared me the reminder of how much energy was going into my body and made that first mouthful seem a lot less daunting. It shouldn't have worked, and for the most part, it didn't, but on one occasion, it did.

Two days before leaving for Wellington, and almost four weeks since having that inaugural feed of mince, mashed potatoes, and peas, I finally found a way to put food in my mouth and eat it. It only happened once, and it was only one slice of peach, but even that felt huge after so long of eating nothing.

I must have felt particularly ballsy that day because a few hours later, I took another stand against anorexia. After tensing my body every few minutes of every day for the past four weeks, I finally decided that enough was enough. If eating the slice of peach at breakfast was a victory in my battle to experience pleasure, now I was making a case to exist without so much self-inflicted pain.

By tensing up whenever I felt guilty, I knew I was putting myself through so much unnecessary strife for such brief moments of peace. I'd always known how irrational it was, but until this point, I hadn't had the mental strength to initiate the change.

Initially, I tried stopping my tensing ritual there and then cold turkey, but as you might expect, that lasted all of about ten minutes. After eating the slice of peach that morning, I already felt guilty enough, so resisting the urge to remove that guilt was simply a step too far.

In the end, I guess anorexia and I made some kind of compromise. Wellington was my last chance to get better, so I knew that if I couldn't make the change now, I'd have to do whatever it took to make it then. So, for my remaining days in Hastings Hospital, I'd tense my body as much as I felt necessary, but once I left, I promised myself I would never do it again. Getting transferred to Wellington was my new line in the sand, and once I crossed it, there would be no going back. It was an ambitious promise, but to this day, it is a promise that's been kept.

For the first time in almost a month, there was progress, and after months of either stagnating or going backwards, that was just enough to keep the hope of my recovery alive. With the move to Wellington now just around the corner, I knew I'd need every sliver of that hope I could find.

Beth Averill (Mum)

We weren't allowed to travel to Wellington with Harry. He went in a car with his CAFS team, and all we could do was follow a few cars behind.

Earlier that day, we were asked to sign legal documents relinquishing our parental rights to decisions regarding his care. This effectively made Harry a 'ward of the state'. Doing this felt so wrong, but we tried to maintain faith in the system and trust that any decisions made would be the right ones for our son.

The doctors had me seriously drugged up for the trip to Wellington, so I don't remember much of the journey. From what I gather, I spent most of it asleep, and when I wasn't sleeping, I was curled up in the fetal position bawling my eyes out.

I'm not sure if the drugs had worn off by the time we arrived, but I remember exactly what happened when I first walked through the doors.

Ten

LIFE IN THE CAPITAL

THE FIRST THING I saw was a guy down the end of the corridor talking to a teddy bear. I couldn't hear what he was saying, and from what I could tell, the teddy bear's mouth wasn't moving, but the guy clearly thought it was talking back. I may have just entered a psych ward, but I decided to give him the benefit of the doubt. He must have got his hands on a telepathic teddy bear.

A nurse led me down the main corridor before steering me into a small room with a couple of chairs. I sat next to my dietitian from CAFS, who then handed me a bottle of Fortisip. She told me I'd missed lunch and wouldn't be getting a new tube put in my nose until later that afternoon. That meant unless I drank what was in the bottle, I wouldn't be getting any food on board until dinner. Either I drank it myself, or my body went the next few hours without. For the first time in weeks, the ball was in my court.

The dietitian knew what I was thinking, and given my track record, she probably knew how slim my chances of finishing it were. So, almost as a parting gift to me before heading back to Hawke's Bay, she said it was okay if I didn't drink it all. As long as I had a mouthful, she'd get off my case and consider the job done.

After hearing this, you might expect that I just did the bare minimum and took the smallest sip she'd let me get away with. After all, why would I create more guilt than I needed to? That's definitely what the dietitian was expecting, and I probably expected the same of myself, too. Surprisingly, that's not at all what happened.

I'm not sure if it was the telepathic teddy bear or the general vibe of the strange new place I found myself in, but I wanted to get out of there and go home as soon as possible. Unfortunately, I knew there was only one way that would happen, and my only ticket out was the Fortisip bottle in my hand. The ball was in my court, and for the first time in a long time, I decided to act rationally.

I closed my eyes, lifted the bottle to my mouth, and essentially inhaled its contents. Then, just like after sculling the liquid breakfast in Ruatoria, I almost instantly wished I hadn't. Like the flick of a switch, my stomach filled with liquid and my mind filled with guilt. It was the best and worst way to start the next stage of my recovery and a stark reminder of why making the wrong decision was so much easier than making the right one. I put my head in my hands and broke down in tears.

***

After half an hour of trying to pull myself together, the dietitian took me across the corridor into another room. Sitting in a big circle of chairs were my parents, the rest of the CAFS team, and about four others who I assumed must be the head doctors and nurses of the Unit. They all seemed friendly enough, and after being introduced to them, the dietitian and I sat down in the remaining seats of the circle.

Then the adults in the room started talking about me, and I couldn't help but feel like they were talking about someone else. It can't have been me they were talking about; the boy who'd hardly eaten anything for six weeks and couldn't go a few minutes without tensing his body; the boy who ignored the instructions of hospital staff and needed 24/7 supervision; the boy who understood his irrationalities yet also never failed to act on them; one of the most complex cases of anorexia that they'd ever seen, all in the form of a fourteen-year-old boy.

How was that me? How had my life come to that when it all seemed so easy such a short time ago? I'd been your typical happy-go-lucky kid: always happy, always smiling, always looking forward to the life I had ahead of me. All I'd done that year was start trying to build myself a better future, so how had it all gone so wrong so quickly?

None of it felt real, and if it was, it certainly didn't feel like I was living a life that belonged to me. It was like being in some kind of cruel simulation where the cap on my misfortunes had been lifted, and all the variables that used to apply to my life had changed.

For most of that conversation, I just sat there feeling sorry for myself, thinking about the drink I'd just sculled, or for the most part, both. I nodded or murmured the odd yes or no when required, but apart from that, I may as well have been someplace else. Eventually, the CAFS team said their goodbyes and my parents and I were left to be shown around the Unit.

The main corridor was covered in all sorts of colourful artwork made by previous patients. This gave the place a weirdly inviting feel, even though it was clearly the last place anyone wanted to be invited. After passing several closed doors, we eventually arrived in an open space with a kitchen, two dining tables, a couple of couches and a TV. It opened into separate courtyards at either end, one with a basketball hoop and the other with a garden. Through another doorway was what they called the movie room, complete with blackout curtains, comfy-looking couches, and a massive flatscreen on the wall. All in all, it was as good of a setting as one could hope for given such undesirable circumstances.

There were about twenty people scattered throughout this space. The teenagers were clearly the patients, and the rest were either nurses or support workers. Unlike the hospital I'd come from, none of the staff were in scrubs, and not one of them had a stethoscope around their neck. Instead, they were dressed in everyday clothes, and rather than checking the patients' hearts, they seemed to be checking how they were feeling.

The other patients said hello as we walked past, and a couple even introduced themselves. They all seemed busy doing something, and to my surprise, none of it seemed particularly abnormal. Some were watching TV, some were doing crosswords, some were writing or drawing in notebooks, and the rest just sat there chatting. Granted, one was chatting to his teddy bear, but again, I decided to let that one slide.

From there, a nurse unlocked a pair of big red doors and led us through to the Unit's bedroom and bathroom wing. After turning a corner and reaching the end of another corridor, we eventually arrived in what she said was my new bedroom. The nurse went through and labelled all of my possessions, confiscated my cell phone and anything sharp, and then watched as my parents and I made my bed and set up my room. Once finished, she gave my parents a not-so-subtle hint to bugger off and leave me to it.

Beth Averill (Mum)

The Unit looked like a prison from the outside, and we had to be ushered through a series of locked doors to reach the meeting room.

During the meeting, a steady stream of patients peered in at us from the main corridor. Seeing the state of them was a real eye-opener for us – we realised Harry would be exposed to things no parent wants their child to see.

They eventually asked us to leave so Harry could attempt dinner. When we came back an hour or so later, we found ourselves locked outside. I remember feeling totally helpless at this point – it was a fitting end to a dreadful day. We got used to the security system after a few weeks, but I never got used to seeing Harry in that environment.

After saying goodbye to him the following morning, I felt like we'd abandoned him with a bunch of strangers. For him to be so far from home, family, and friends in such a vulnerable state of mind seemed so cruel.

The goodbyes never got easier.

***

Patients inside the Unit could be on one of four levels of supervision. For my first month or so, I found myself on level one, which, unsurprisingly, was the one with the least amount of freedom.

As was the case back in Hastings, there were a set of eyes on me around the clock, and the only exception was when I was taking a shower or doing my business. Even then, a nurse or support worker stood a couple of metres away with their back turned, listening to my every move.

Each morning, I woke up to a support worker sitting in my doorway staring in at me. This would have been unnerving for most people, but for me, it was definitely more appealing than waking up with the room to myself. Anorexia was desperate to maintain its control, and after being under supervision for so long, I was scared what it would make me do when it had me to itself.

Once dressed, I'd usually have to watch as a nurse made me breakfast. I'd then spend the next half an hour staring at the food in front of me while occasionally picking at it to keep any onlookers interested. If a staff member ever piled on the pressure, sometimes I'd lift the food to my mouth like I was about to eat it. It was really just an act because, for that first month, no food even came close to being swallowed. At that stage, a repeat of my peach slice heroics seemed a long way off.

Each unsuccessful meal attempt was followed by a trip to the medical room to be fed down the tube. Unlike in Hastings, where the Fortisip flowed slowly from a stand, the nurses here emptied each bottle down the tube all at once. This mimicked the feeling of eating a meal quickly and got me used to the sensation of my stomach growing full. It was a smart idea, and as tough as it made those first few days, the mental assault accompanying each feed gradually lost its intensity.

Something else that lost its intensity during the first month was the pressure I felt to hold my body in a tense. There were several things about being in the Unit that I think made this possible.

For one, it helped to have a change of scene. Habits are often attached to settings, and finding myself somewhere new did seem to lower the volume of those compulsive thoughts. No one at the Unit had ever witnessed my tensing ritual, and because of that, I didn't feel like anyone expected me to start. There was never any recognition that my behaviour had changed, and this prevented me from remembering how much I had to feel guilty about. In this case, a complete absence of praise was just what I needed.

Compared to life in a hospital bed, there was also much more going on around me. As well as being surrounded by other patients and staff, I had to participate in the Unit's Day Programme. This ran between breakfast and dinner on weekdays and stimulated my mind like a hospital room never could.

For patients in the programme, breakfast was followed by a couple of hours of 'school'. The Unit had a classroom and a fantastic teacher but apart from that, calling it a school is a bit of a stretch. Having the motivation to learn requires having belief in your future, and for most of us patients, our futures were hardly visible, let alone worth studying for. Even if we could somehow find the motivation to work, our states of mind were hardly conducive to productivity. Most of us just sat there staring off into space, and if we weren't doing that, it was usually because our heads were in our hands and our eyes were full of tears.

The goal was to prevent us from slipping too far behind other students our age, but that would be a tough ask no matter how good the teacher was. Instead of assigning us work based on our year at school, she had to consider the limitations of our current emotional states. For most of us, that meant having the work ethic and productivity of about the average five-year-old.

On my first day, the teacher asked me to create a poster about myself – or perhaps more accurately, my former self. It took me that whole first week to finish, and even then, what I came up with was far from flash. After all that time, all I produced was a piece of paper with my name scribbled in the centre and a few cut-outs from a rugby magazine glued around the outside. It was an appalling effort and something I know my five-year-old self would have been ashamed of creating.

School was always followed by lunch, and between lunch and dinner, the staff organised a range of activities for us to take part in. As well as keeping our minds stimulated, they were designed to help us come to grips with our feelings and, if possible, express them. There were all sorts of activities, but the following seemed to be the most common when I was there: music therapy, poetry, flax (harakeke) weaving, singing waiata (Māori songs), pottery and painting.

This may seem a bit airy-fairy, and if I'm being honest, I was never the most enthusiastic of participants, but giving those activities a go always made me feel better. I'm not sure if they helped me make sense of the thoughts in my head or just allowed me to escape them, but it felt good to be kept busy for a change. If there was one thing for sure, it beat twiddling my thumbs in a hospital bed.

We'd usually get through a few of these activities by dinnertime and would then spend the rest of each day as we pleased (sort of). Each patient had their own restrictions, but the ones applying to me always seemed the most draconian. I wasn't officially on bed rest like I was in Hastings, but I may as well have been because occasions on my feet were still few and far between. Unless I had good reason to move from one seat to another, I was ordered to stay where I was.

Then there were the twenty-minute 'rest periods' following each of my meals. Wherever I was during these, be that in the classroom or outside in the courtyard, I had to sit with my feet up on a chair until the time was up. I'm still not entirely sure what this was meant to achieve, but it was certainly a massive inconvenience for me and anyone who had to give up their seat for my feet.

These restrictions may seem petty, especially now that my physical health was less of an issue, but the staff enforced them like the fate of the world depended on it. Each time I stood up unannounced, they reacted as if I'd just pulled out a gun, and if I took my feet off the seat even a minute earlier than instructed, they'd lift them straight back up, sometimes with force.

As unnecessary as all this may seem, I did begin to appreciate how strict they were with me. They made it clear the boundaries they set were not allowed to be crossed, with no exceptions. I could try to get onto my feet without permission, but within seconds I would have staff on my case sitting me back down. I could try to take my feet off the couch after eighteen minutes instead of twenty, but every single time, I would be caught. There were no opportunities to stretch the rules, and because of that, anorexia had much less room to manipulate my behaviour.

Being transferred to Wellington had so far been the fresh start that I needed to make a change, and although eating still felt a long way off, I was relieved to have finally stopped putting my body through so much pain. If I let that door open again, I knew I may never get another chance to close it.

***

If I didn't appreciate before how lucky I was to have such a supportive family, I certainly did now that I was in the Unit. While some patients battled for weeks without seeing or talking to their families, mine lived almost four hours away yet still found a way to visit every weekend. On a few occasions, Mum even came down midweek when she had time off work.

No matter how many reasons I gave them not to return, they always did, and with just as much hope and positivity as the time before. No matter how often I let them down, their love and support for me held firm. Even when I offered absolutely nothing back in return, they were always there, and no matter what I did or didn't do, I knew they always would be. I simply can't overstate the influence this had on my recovery.

While visiting, they usually stayed in what was known as the Unit's Whānau (Family) Room. This was attached to the outskirts of the complex and was available for patients' families at no cost. It came with few amenities, and my parents had to stock its kitchen drawers, but as far as they were concerned, it did the job. Fortunately for us, it was almost always available.

Weekends were always relatively quiet in the Unit, so to have family staying just outside the main doors was a huge bonus. I couldn't leave the Unit for my first six weeks but was allowed to join them in the Whānau Room for a few hours at a time. It was as close to an escape from the Unit as I got, and the only time I wasn't being watched by someone getting paid to do so.

Their visits were the highlight of my weeks, and because of this, anorexia did almost everything it could to ruin them. Having lost its ability to make me tense up like a maniac, the illness was struggling more than ever to keep me under its control. It no longer had the power to put me through pain, and because of this, it started doubling down on its efforts to deprive me of pleasure.

Whether it was eating food or spending time with family, I felt undeserving of every enjoyable experience available. Whenever an opportunity for enjoyment arose, it was like my thoughts automatically switched into guilt-generating loops of self-criticism. From here, any sense of self-worth I had could be destroyed in seconds; hospital is making me lazy; I'm losing my edge; I'm getting unfit, fat, overindulgent, and eventually, I'm a worthless piece of crap who deserves nothing that's good in the world. I'd convince myself I wasn't even worthy of my own family's company.

Jumping to these conclusions may seem extreme, but unfortunately, anorexia has never been one to beat around the bush. I could be sitting in the Whānau Room quite calmly watching TV with my parents and a minute later be rocking back and forward with my knees pressed to my chest and my head in my hands.

My visits to the Whānau Room all started off pleasantly enough, but they all ended the same way: a nurse taking me away, a tearful goodbye, and another opportunity to enjoy myself missed. To give you an idea of what this looked like from the outside, here's something that my little brother wrote after he and Mum came down one weekend.

Oscar (23/11/2013 – aged 10)

Last weekend I went to Wellington with Mum to visit Harry for the first time. When I first saw him, he was still mumbling but was better than I expected and even smiled a couple of times. As the day went on, he got worse and worse. By the end of the night, I was shocked at what I saw and started to really see how hard it is for him. The next day he was pretty much the same and by the end of the day he was really bad. As usual, we had to leave him on a bad note.

When they weren't visiting, my family rang the Unit every night to chat. I never offered much down my end of the line, but that didn't seem to matter. Whether it was my parents, grandparents, or brothers, just hearing their voices and what they'd been getting up to was enough to remind me where I came from and what awaited me when I returned.

As tough as it was to hear how much life I was missing out on, this motivated me more than anything to get my life back on track. The outside world continued to go on without me, and until I earned back my place within it, I remained trapped in a world more akin to The Truman Show than real life.

Eleven

DRAFTING SHEEP

After ticking off my first month in the Rangatahi Unit, life started feeling less like an R18 horror movie with possessive demons and more like an R16 with a few zombies. Waking up as me each day was still scary as heck, but a few cracks of light were starting to break through the darkness of my mind. The once ferocious guilt was losing its edge, and the shadow hanging over me wasn't quite as dark and heavy as it was before.

It had been two months since I'd started taking medication back in Hastings, so the timing of these improvements suggests drugs were at least partly responsible. It took slightly longer than expected for me to notice their effects, but as their doses ramped up, these became increasingly obvious. The pile of pills placed in front of me each day continued growing, and with that, my mind became a slightly more tolerable place to be.

As transformative as those drugs might have been, they can't take all the credit for my improved state of mind. Since arriving in the Unit, I'd been assigned a psychologist to meet with a few times each week. In the past four weeks, she'd taught me more about anorexia and how to fight it than any dose of drugs ever could.

It might be different now that I've had years to reflect, but when I first entered the Unit, I didn't have a clue how to make sense of the chaos between my ears. I could feel the guilt, the fear, and the dread, but in no way did I understand the anorexic inner workings that put them there. Like anyone else, I'd always assumed the thoughts in my head were my own – not someone else's, and certainly not the product of the illness inside my mind. Because of this, I'd never known to do anything other than listen to what those thoughts said.

It wasn't until I started having sessions with the psychologist that I learned how to separate fact from fiction within my mind. To do this, I first had to recognise that only some of the thoughts in my head were my own. The rest, which at this stage were most of them, were the creations of the illness I'd developed – anorexia. They may have all felt like thoughts that belonged to me, and in reality, they did, but until I learned to differentiate myself from the illness, beating it would be all but impossible.

Once I'd got my head around that, the next step was figuring out how to tell one type of thought from the other. This involved a lot of soul-searching, but in the end, I managed to come up with a pretty simple criteria: if a thought has anything to do with putting myself through pain or depriving myself of pleasure, it probably comes from anorexia, and if it doesn't, it's probably my own. From there, it was just a case of learning to push the anorexic thoughts aside and listening only to 'Harry's thoughts' instead. That seems simple enough, right? Not quite.

Trying to sort through every thought that enters your mind is a bit like trying to draft sheep. The sheep are racing through the gates, and your job is to decide which of the two holding pens to direct them into as they pass. Not only do you need to differentiate one type of sheep from the other, but once you've done that, you need to steer each of them into the right pen. Trying to figure out which thoughts were mine and which were anorexia's was hard enough. Figuring out how to push the anorexic ones aside was another challenge altogether.

Since arriving at the unit, I'd got pretty good at ignoring the anorexic thoughts telling me to exercise, tense, or somehow push my body to its limits. These were the thoughts stemming from the 'pain' side of the anorexic coin I've mentioned before. Now I'd got the hang of that, my next job was dealing with the thoughts convincing me I was undeserving of enjoyment. In other words, it was now time to deal with the 'pleasure' side of that coin. This proved to be a lot more challenging.

Fortunately, I started making breakthroughs in this domain in the weeks leading up to Christmas, and they came in the form of eating food.

***

The guilt always seemed to get worse as the day went on, so at first, it was just a spoonful of rice bubbles at breakfast. The following day, it was two spoonfuls with a bite of toast. Then I found a way to turn it up a notch. The following week, I got down most of breakfast each day and had a few bites of lunch and dinner, too. The trend continued, and on Christmas Eve, I finished my first full meal since the night I arrived at Hastings Hospital ten weeks earlier.

How did I do it? The easy answer is that I put the food in my mouth, chewed it for a bit and swallowed, but you've probably guessed as much. Like most people, I found that part of the process relatively straightforward. What wasn't so easy were the mental gymnastics that made those actions possible. That's where the answer to how I did it gets a lot more complicated.

Unlike learning how to stop myself from tensing, making myself eat involved initiating an action rather than just preventing one. To prevent myself from tensing up, all I had to do was ignore the anorexic thoughts telling me to do so. This was much easier said than done, but by keeping myself distracted, I hadn't acted on those compulsions since arriving in the Unit.

Yet when trying to make myself eat, just ignoring the thoughts telling me not to wasn't enough. I could ignore those thoughts all I liked, but unfortunately, that wasn't enough to get the food off my plate and down my throat. To make that happen, I had to not only ignore those anorexic thoughts but challenge them and, through doing so, generate my own thoughts – the kind of thoughts that made eating seem like something worth doing. Only then could I initiate the relatively straightforward process of putting the food in my mouth and eating it.

Believe me, I can appreciate how outlandish this sounds. Speaking of anorexia as if it was some kind of evil homunculus inside my brain is weird enough. To then say I had an imaginary debate with it to make myself eat is downright bonkers. I get all that, and I can assure you, I felt bonkers doing it. Yet by imagining anorexia as something separate from myself with its own thoughts and motivations, it shifted from something that felt part of me to something I could examine objectively and fight back against. So, as weird as it sounds, establishing this kind of framework inside my mind did wonders for my recovery.

Here's an example of how that process might have played out in my head when it came to eating:

Anorexia: Don't eat.

Harry: Everybody else eats, why shouldn't I?

Anorexia: You've done nowhere near enough exercise, and you're getting fat, lazy and unfit. Eating will only make you feel worse about yourself.

Harry: How is eating going to change anything? If I don't eat, I'll still be fed the same amount of energy down the tube. Besides, even if I am getting fat, lazy and unfit, that's not something I have control over now that I'm in hospital. I have no logical reason to feel guilty.

Anorexia: If you want to be successful in life, you need to make sacrifices other people aren't willing to make. The rules that apply to other people can't apply to you, and according to your rules, you haven't done nearly enough to deserve to eat.

Harry: That makes no sense. Making sacrifices may lead to success in some cases, but by continuing not to eat, all I'm doing is making things worse. Until I start eating, I'll never be able to leave hospital, let alone be successful. Besides, the sooner I eat, the sooner I'll be allowed to exercise again. Isn't that what you want?

*Harry: *eats**

*Anorexia: *gives Harry another beating between his ears**

*Harry: *promises himself he'll never eat again**

Like I said, it's complicated.

***

As a reward for all this progress, the staff agreed to shift me from level one supervision to level two. Life at level two wasn't much different to what I was used to, but it did come with a few perks. For one, I was finally allowed to leave the Unit for the weekly outing on Friday afternoons.

My first outing was two weeks before Christmas. It was a stinking hot summer day, so a few staff members took us to a local park. That may not seem like much, but after so long cooped up in hospital, for me it was like being taken to Disneyland. Seeing such wide-open spaces filled with so many shades of green was almost overstimulating, and I could have quite happily sat there all day like a weirdo feeling the grass between my fingers and toes.

The park had a playground, and although I was the only patient remotely close to a playground-appropriate age, I was also the only one not allowed to use it. Fortunately, watching the others provided more than enough entertainment.

In the centre of the playground was a massive climbing pyramid made of rope. As soon as we arrived, one of the older patients made a beeline straight to the top of it. The staff found this concerning for obvious reasons, but it wasn't until an hour later that her position ten metres up in the air became a problem. It was time to head back to the Unit, and she refused to get down.

No matter how many times the staff asked, the girl stood her ground, and when they started dishing out threats, her only response was a raised middle finger. The situation always had the potential to turn serious, but in the meantime, the rest of us patients were getting the best entertainment we'd had in months. It wasn't often someone got the upper hand over the staff, and the complete arrogance she was giving them only made it better.

After so long in the Unit, she was milking her moment of power for all it was worth, and as stressful as that must have been for the staff, we patients couldn't get enough of it. I had a smile on my dial for the first time in weeks, and the other patients cheered her on like she was some kind of hero. To us, I guess she was.

After several failed negotiation attempts and ignored threats, the staff eventually gave up and called emergency services. A few minutes later, and to the complete amusement of the rest of us, a fire truck wailed towards us from the other side of town. As soon as it arrived, a firefighter moved toward her on the end of the truck's hydraulic ladder. Still unconvinced, the girl stayed where she was with a raised middle finger, an outstretched tongue, and a look of utter disdain across her face.

It wasn't until the fireman was a metre away from her that she made her move, and her timing could not have been better. With more arrogance than I've seen in my entire life, she casually made her way down to the ground, grabbed her bag, whipped it over her shoulder, and walked nonchalantly back towards the car park.

Needless to say, her next few weeks in the Unit weren't much fun.

***

The following week's outing was a trip to the beach, and after once again not being the one to have emergency services called on them, my restrictions were lifted just in time for Christmas. It may have required some persuasion from my parents, but the staff eventually agreed to let me spend Christmas Day outside the Unit with family. To them, it was an unnecessary risk. To us, it was another huge opportunity for progress.

As soon as Mum heard the news, she arranged for my family to stay at a place that needed housesitting over that period. The house was big enough for the whole family – grandparents and dog included – and was on a big section with plenty of room to kick a ball around. In other words, it was perfect.

When my parents picked me up on Christmas morning, they saw me without a tube in my nose for the first time in a couple of months. Mum burst into tears, and Dad gave me the kind of pat on the back he reserves for special occasions. They told me it was the best Christmas present they could have asked for.

This made it a bit of an anti-climax when I admitted it had actually come out by mistake. I was getting dressed earlier that morning when the tube caught itself on one of my shirt buttons. Without realising, I then pulled the shirt down over my head and yanked the whole thing out of my nose and onto the floor. The only reason it hadn't been replaced was because it was Christmas, so I'd been able to convince the nurses to leave it for the afternoon shift to deal with. Mum and Dad were visibly disappointed, but agreed that the rest of the family didn't need to hear that part of the story.

My parents knew I needed to be kept busy, so we started opening presents as soon as we arrived at the house. I hadn't had the chance to do any Christmas shopping, so the only gifts I dished out were things I'd made inside the Unit. There were homemade cards, baskets weaved out of flax (kete), unsightly objects made of clay, and for Mum and Dad, the poem I wrote below. No one seemed particularly stoked with these presents – aside from a very emotional Mum – but hey, at least they were cheap.

To Mum and Dad,
You were there for me
when I needed you most,
when I hit rock bottom
off a stormy coast.
You helped me see
that dim, dull light,
through all the thoughts
I had to fight.
Love Harry

The rest of the day went far from smoothly, but on the whole, my first outing with family was deemed a success. I got through a colossal Christmas lunch, played rugby with my brothers without turning it into an exercise routine, and perhaps most surprisingly, there were even a few occasions when I talked in sentences rather than grunts.

For the first time in a long time, I showed glimpses of the boy I was before. For the first time ever, it was no longer a question of *if* that boy would eventually return to his family for good, but *when.*

Beth Averill

Christmas Day felt like such a breakthrough. Not only did Harry give us a few smiles, but he even did a bit of talking and ate a big Christmas lunch (pudding included!).

I saw a few glimmers of the old Harry, and for the first time, I started genuinely believing he might get back to being that person one day. The poem he wrote for us meant so much and probably remains one of the best presents I've ever received.

Unfortunately, things went downhill very quickly after lunch. Harry spent the next couple of hours pacing up and down the hallway or standing with his head pressed hard against the wall. We were under strict instructions to take Harry back to the Unit (or call the police) if he started behaving strangely, so after a couple of hours of trying to snap him out of it, we reluctantly took him back early.

***

Thankfully, the tube didn't need to be put back in until lunchtime the following day. After being dropped back at the Unit, I ate all my Christmas dinner and even managed to eat breakfast the following morning. Getting through another lunch was a step too far, but heading into 2014, the trajectory of my recovery was clearly heading in the right direction. Anorexia was losing grip within my mind, and as it did, I was regaining a grip of my own.

There weren't any more major breakthroughs in the week that followed, but by holding on to the ones already made, there was progress all the same. I ate most of every meal in front of me, and if I didn't, you can guarantee I did everything I could to challenge the anorexic thoughts stopping me. My side of the argument continued growing stronger, and I began seeing more and more of those thoughts for the nonsensical lies they were.

By early January 2014, a return to normality looked less like a pipe dream and more like a not-so-distant future. I'd challenged anorexia more in the past month than the rest of its existence, and although my life was still far from pleasant, all signs seemed to point towards a better tomorrow than today.

Then I relapsed, and all hope of that future was gone.

Twelve

FINDING THE SWITCH

RECOVERING FROM A MENTAL illness doesn't happen linearly. For me, it was like being on a rollercoaster that got bumpier and less predictable the further I got down the track. The longer I was able to hold on, the more fiercely it tried to throw me off course. The more I did to fight it, the harder it fought back.

Having achieved so much in the past month, I suppose it was inevitable that I'd eventually have some kind of setback. I'd been eating most of what was put in front of me, ignoring the compulsive thoughts entering my head, and in light of all this, I'd started genuinely believing a return to normal was within my reach. Naively, I assumed my momentum would continue and that all the progress I'd made would be there to stay. Unfortunately, I was about to learn that when it comes to mental illness, progress can be undone a lot faster than it can be earned.

The day started like every other day had that week. I'd eaten breakfast and lunch, I'd managed to get some work done at school, and mentally, I was feeling better than I had in months. I was still no more than a four out of ten on the happiness scale, but compared to what I was used to, even that felt like a win. It wasn't until the afternoon that life dealt me my reality check.

If before I'd been dealing with anorexia, that afternoon came the arrival of what felt like anorexia on steroids. Seemingly out of nowhere, my mind plunged back into a state of despair, and within hours, the guilt was as pervasive as it had ever been before. I felt my consciousness constrict into one tight knot of darkness – within that space, anorexic thoughts were the only ones I could hear. My month of progress was undone, and just like that, the future I'd only just started believing in had vanished.

Once dinnertime came around, eating anything off my plate felt about as manageable as eating the ceramic plate itself. It was like my mind had already been made up for me, and this time around, no amount of mental gymnastics seemed able to reverse it. The longer I sat there trying to find the motivation, the further it seemed to slip away. The more I thought about taking that first mouthful, the more convincing anorexia's case for abstinence became.

When I failed to eat breakfast or lunch the following day, the staff put the tube back in and decided to put me on bed rest. This may seem pointless – after all, they could feed me all the energy I needed down the tube – but they knew from my time in Hastings Hospital that I hated lying in bed more than anything else. For that reason alone, it was the perfect punishment, and the way they saw it, the fastest way to get me eating again. Until I found a way to eat, they would keep me trapped inside my own little version of hell.

As usual, the staff stuck to their word, so for the next three and a half days, I lay in bed with a support worker watching me like a hawk from my bedroom doorway. To make matters worse, they also confiscated my MP3 player, which I'd been listening to whenever I got the chance. I didn't yet have the concentration to read books, so this left me with only a notepad, pen, and my thoughts to keep me busy. As you can probably imagine, that didn't make for a pleasant few days.

Like in Hastings, the sense of entrapment I felt on bed rest was two-fold. Not only did I feel trapped inside my mind, but my movements were so restricted that I may as well have been wearing a straitjacket. This made the anorexic thoughts even harder than usual to ignore. Acting on those compulsions was the only way I could relieve myself from guilt, and on bed rest, relief from guilt was the only form of escape I could get.

If there was a positive about that period, it was that, unlike back in Hastings, I was able to ignore any thoughts telling me to hold my body in a tense. I'm sure the drugs I was on played a part in this, but again, they can't take all the credit. As enticing as it was to tense up and experience the guilt-free moments that followed, I was determined to not slip further than I already had. It may have taken every ounce of willpower I could find, and there were plenty of times I came dangerously close to giving in, but ultimately, the promise I'd made to myself was kept.

To distract myself, I spent most of those days scribbling or stabbing into my notepad with a pen. That may sound rather violent, and I assure you it was, but it was also remarkably cathartic. Fortunately, only one notebook was harmed in the process.

Here's a poem I found jotted down amongst the scribbles, rips and holes left over from those attacks. It was the only coherent combination of words I could find, but I think it does a pretty good job of summing up what I felt at the time.

the inside of my eyelids

is the only thing I see,

I'm trapped inside a mind

in which I don't want to be.

let me out, let me be free,

so I can live a normal life,

be the person my family loves

and grow stronger amongst the strife.

01/2014

***

I've mentioned before that a step back is sometimes what it takes to find a new way forward, and this relapse is a prime example. As tough as those few days back on bed rest were, they also led to the most crucial moment of my recovery.

In all nine years that have followed, not a day has gone by where I haven't looked back and appreciated the breakthroughs that were made. It was when everything in my life changed forever and never returned. A sad story finished, and from that moment on, a new story – a story of redemption – began. After so long walking aimlessly in the dark, it was the moment I finally found the switch.

When I woke up on bed rest for the third morning in a row, it certainly didn't feel like I was about to turn my life around. In fact, I still felt as miserable as ever. In those past few days, all the progress I'd made since arriving in the Unit seemed to have been undone, and as far as I could tell, there was nothing I could have done to stop it. I'd tried my best to challenge the anorexic thoughts in my head, but yet again, my best just hadn't been enough. Anorexia had recaptured a monopoly inside my mind, and I was merely a passenger on its endless quest to ruin my life.

As with the days prior, the arrival of breakfast in bed that morning felt far from luxurious. In typically brutal fashion, pessimistic and guilt-ridden thoughts flooded my mind, and within minutes, I'd already come to accept that I wouldn't be eating a thing. As much as I knew I should be, and as irrational as I knew it was not to, yet again, I just couldn't find a way to make it happen. The anorexic thoughts were too convincing, the accompanying guilt was too intense, and amongst all of that, my own thoughts couldn't be heard.

My memory of what happened next has undoubtedly been altered over the years, but from what I recall, it all started with me reflecting on how screwed I was. There I was, sitting in a psychiatric hospital at the age of fourteen. Health care professionals surrounded me because I wasn't safe in my own company, I had a tube in my nose because I couldn't eat enough to stay alive, and to really hammer the message home, I was almost certainly going to miss the start of my second year at high school. Everyone else my age was out there living life and growing up, and all I was doing was falling further and further behind.

It wasn't the first time I'd realised how screwed I was. In fact, I'd probably had that thought thousands of times in the past six months. The only difference this time around were the thoughts and feelings that followed.

Usually, reflecting on my situation would have made me start feeling sorry for myself. My mind would sink into a deeper state of despair, tears would start to fall, and only once they'd run out would I find a way to pull myself together, lift my head out of my hands and carry on. I'd force myself to believe that by 'hanging in there' and 'trusting the process' as everyone told me to, one day I'd wake up and the nightmare would be over. As long as I held onto hope, one day, everything would be okay again.

This time was different. Instead of feeling sorry for myself and discouraged by the situation I found myself in, this time, all I felt was anger. At first, I didn't know what to be angry at. Should I be angry at my parents for bringing me into the world, giving me the wrong genes or somehow raising me wrong? Should I be angry at society for pressuring me into such a state and letting me slip through the cracks of the healthcare system? Should I be angry at myself for making all the wrong decisions and not asking for help when I needed it? Or, if there is a God, should I be angry at Him or Her for allowing everything to play out the way it had?

The longer I thought, the angrier I became and the more I yearned for someone to blame for everything that had gone wrong. The past few days had been the final straw, and as I stared at the seemingly inedible breakfast in front of me, I decided once and for all that enough was enough.

I could no longer accept that what I was going through was all just part of my fate and that one day, mental illness might leave me alone. I'd run out of patience for that, and if I'm being honest, I felt like I was running out of time. My nightmare had already gone on for too long, and I knew that the longer it continued, the harder it would be to wake up from it. I needed redemption, and for that to happen, I knew that something drastic about my life needed to change.

That's when something inside me switched. It was like an epiphany, yet the ground-breaking truth I saw was one I should have seen months ago. Everyone around me had seen it, yet until that point, anorexia had kept the wool pulled over my eyes.

I realised there was no point getting angry at myself, the world, anyone else who lives within it, nor was there any point getting angry at some kind of higher power. Nothing that had already happened could be undone, yet crucially, I also realised that nothing about my situation needed to be permanent. It was entirely within my power to change my situation, if only I could find a way to change myself. Change myself, and everything outside my control would eventually fall into place.

There was only one thing holding me back, and in that moment, I could finally see it for what it was. It may seem obvious in hindsight or to anyone else, but at the time, I remember it seeming nothing short of profound. The source of all my problems, and the common denominator in everything that had ruined my life, was and always had been, the bully between my ears: anorexia. So, if I was going to be angry at anything, I needed to be angry at that. Get rid of anorexia, and not only would I get my life back, but I'd destroy the very thing that took it from me in the first place.

Realising that changed everything. Just like that, my anger had found its home, and I'd suddenly unearthed all the motivation I'd ever need to get my life back on track. The only thing I needed to change was myself, and the only thing about myself I needed to change was anorexia. I could finally see the illness for the enemy it was, and now I'd established that, I could finally become the hero of my own story.

***

It may seem ridiculous, but up until this point, part of me still saw value in keeping that 'no pain, no gain' mindset I'd adopted a year ago. After so long obsessed with sacrificing my present in the hope of setting up my future, the idea that I now needed to become less disciplined to improve my life was so difficult for me to accept. Like a sportsperson told they need to start training less to improve their performance, going easier on myself had always seemed counterintuitive. No matter how irrationally disciplined I'd become, and how costly the resulting behaviours had been, my brain still found a way to make it all feel like progress.

In hindsight, I think this is why my recovery had been so slow and laborious up until this point. Of course, I'd always wanted to get better, but because I still saw value in staying so disciplined, I'd also been remarkably resistant to change. I was fighting so hard to change my behaviour and appear normal on the outside, yet on the inside, I still held onto the 'no pain, no gain' mindset that gave anorexia life. Instead of fighting for a life free of anorexia, I was really just trying to work my life around it. Change felt scary, and a weird comfort came with keeping things the way they were inside my head.

If I'd continued holding onto this approach, I'm sure I'd have eventually found a way to stay alive outside of hospital. I'd have figured out how to eat enough, how to exercise without overdoing it, and maybe even how to enjoy myself every now and again. It would have taken a lot longer to achieve, and the mental gymnastics involved would have been a lot more complex, but eventually, I may have found a way to keep myself alive without destroying anorexia in the process.

I'm sure many people with anorexia have achieved this state, but I'm beyond grateful I stopped trying to get there when I did. Anorexia is impossible to satisfy, and I know that no matter what I did in life, that bully would have always been in the back of my mind demanding more. More discipline, more sacrifice, more pain, and ultimately, less of everything that makes a life worth living. I may have found a way to stay alive, but in the corniest sense, I would have never been truly living. The bully would still be the one pulling the strings between my ears, and I'd have just become a more reluctant puppet. On the inside, I would have always been an anorexic.

That's what made the realisations I had at breakfast that day so special. By getting angry at anorexia and hating it for what it had done to me, I could finally let go of the 'no pain, no gain' mindset it evolved from. My ability to stay disciplined had always felt like part of me I needed to protect, but now it felt like something foreign I had to destroy. It wasn't part of me, it had never helped me, and to get my life back, I needed to move as far away from it as possible. I needed to beat anorexia at its source, and to do that, I needed to completely let that mindset go. Happiness, not success, had to become my priority, and instead of toughening up, I needed to start toughening down. In other words, I needed to start going easier on myself.

Like jumping off a cliff into the unknown, doing so went against every instinct, but I knew it was the only way forward. I didn't want to be anorexic for the rest of my life, and now I'd realised I didn't have to be, change went from something I was afraid of to something I was able to embrace.

The future I'd struggled for so long to believe in was now the only future I was willing to accept, and I was determined to make it my reality. It was no longer a matter of hoping that my situation would improve, it was knowing that I had the power to change it, so if I wanted to get my life back, nothing would be able to stop me. I was going to start bullying the bully, and through doing so, I was going to claim back that space between my ears. It would start with eating the breakfast in front of me, and it wouldn't stop until anorexia was nothing but a distant memory.

I haven't missed a meal since.

Thirteen

SEEING THE LIGHT

WHEN I STARTED HIGH school a year earlier, I changed my entire approach to life because I wanted to grow up and be successful. Adopting a 'no pain, no gain' mindset worked for about a month before anorexia took hold, turned all of my youthful ambition against me and eventually almost killed me. To reverse the damage, I realised now that all I had to do was start living life the way I was before. It was a case of unlearning the things anorexia had taught me and relearning how to make happiness a priority again.

Putting it like that makes it all sound so simple, and nine years on, I often wonder why I hadn't realised it sooner. I guess that's just the nature of mental illness: we can only interpret what's happening to us through our minds, and when our minds aren't working the way they're meant to, it's harder for us to see the reality of our situations. My mind tricked me into believing I was broken beyond repair when, in reality, I was only a change in mindset away from turning it all around.

It may seem like that mindset came to me out of nowhere, but by that point, I'd already gone a long way toward finding it. A few months earlier, my psychologist taught me how to differentiate anorexic thoughts from my own, and ever since then, I'd been imagining anorexia as something separate from myself. Doing this felt strange initially but soon became second nature, and eventually, I didn't see anorexia as an illness but as something evil living inside me. The anorexic thoughts still felt like my own, but by pretending they weren't, I could observe the illness through a more objective lens. I started picking up on its tone, patterns, and with time, the bullyish persona it used to control me.

The process was far from straightforward, and as the past few days of relapse show, sometimes anorexia's identity and mine merged back into one. Yet the longer I tried to think of it as something separate, the further I distanced myself from the 'no pain, no gain' mindset it stemmed from. I slowly teased apart my identity from the bully that had taken over, and eventually, I broke out from under its wing and saw the entire mindset for the counterproductive trap that it was.

Now that I'd seen that, beating anorexia became much less complex. Take eating, for example. Before, every anorexic thought aligned perfectly with that 'no pain, no gain' mindset, so those thoughts always felt more intuitive than my own. Anorexic thoughts had a head start over the rest, so on days when there were lots of them, doing the opposite of what they told me seemed almost impossible.

Having finally let that mindset go, this was no longer the case. The anorexic thoughts all revolved around making some kind of sacrifice, yet with happiness, not success, now my priority, they seemed nowhere near as convincing as before. Instead of debating the logic of those thoughts against my own, now I could reject them based on face value alone. Here's an example of how that process may have played out inside my new and improved mind:

Anorexia: Don't eat.

Harry: Everybody else eats, why shouldn't I?

Anorexia: You've done nowhere near enough exercise, and you're getting fat, lazy and unfit. Eating will only make you feel worse about yourself.

Harry: You're not me, you're anorexia, and that means you're completely full of shit. Whatever you tell me to do, I'm going to do the opposite. I deserve to be happy, and you've already put me through enough pain to last a lifetime. I hate everything about you, and it's time for you to get the hell out of my head.

*Harry: *eats**

*Anorexia: *gives Harry another beating between his ears**

*Harry: *convinces himself it's worth it and promises himself that once lunchtime comes around, he'll do it all over again**

***

It's amazing what can change in a week. After getting that breakfast down in record-breaking time, the staff agreed to take me off bed rest. This was a huge relief, and joining the other patients back in the Day Programme did further wonders for my state of mind. I still had trouble concentrating in school, but there was a sense of purpose to the struggle that wasn't there before. As tough as it was to find focus, like everything else in my life, I was determined to make it easier.

After two days of eating every plate and bowl clean, a nurse took the tube out of my nose for the last time. Each meal seemed to go down easier than the last, and as one week rolled into the next, the milestones kept coming. Level one supervision became level two, and the following week, level two became level three. Gone were the days of 24/7 supervision, and back were the blessed days of using the toilet without company. I still spent most of my days within the sights of a staff member, but even brief moments of independence felt like a massive step forward.

The day after moving to level three, my doctor told me I'd reached my 'target weight'. I was still considered 'underweight' for a boy of my age and height, and mentally, I was still a long way off where I needed to be for hospital discharge, but reaching this milestone was huge in the context of my recovery. With my physical health no longer compromised, the staff reluctantly agreed to let me exercise again.

After not exercising for so long, I felt tremendous pressure to get my fitness back to where it was before. I knew this wasn't something I should want, and I knew it was anorexia making me feel like this, but that didn't make the pressure go away.

As far as I'd come with eating, I'd largely neglected the exercise aspect of my recovery until this point. I'd spent the last few months learning to cope without it, but learning to exercise without pushing my body to its limits was another challenge altogether. Happiness, not success, may have become my priority, but when it came to exercise, plenty of old habits still needed breaking.

Thankfully, the staff knew how difficult this transition would be, so they limited my exercise to three fifteen-minute walks each day. I wasn't allowed to leave the Unit alone, so I usually spent this time walking up and down the main corridor. Moving my legs felt amazing after months of sitting down. Initially, even walking was enough to relieve the guilt for a while.

The only problem was, after a few days, the staff realised I was losing weight. I was already eating an absurd amount of food, so they cut my exercise to just fifteen minutes daily to prevent my weight from slipping further. I wasn't stoked to hear this, but in the end, the staff and I arrived at a compromise. Instead of spending that fifteen-minutes walking, they agreed to let me shoot the basketball outside. In the end, having this extra freedom was both a blessing and a curse. As hard as I tried to keep the intensity down, it didn't take long for me to slip into the 'no pain, no gain' exercise habits of old.

Unlike making myself eat, I found exercising at lower intensities much harder to justify. If I didn't eat, I either got fed through a tube again or starved. If I pushed my body to its limits, all that happened was I got fitter. Anyone on the street would tell you that getting fitter is a good thing, so ignoring these kinds of anorexic thoughts was a lot more difficult. The promise of that post-work-out high was far too tempting, and as much as I wanted to relax and enjoy the experience, what started as shooting hoops quickly turned into shuttle sprints with a ball.

The staff initially did all they could to make me slow it down, but after a few days, they must have agreed to turn a blind eye. They saw the pain in my eyes as I raced around the courtyard, but they also saw the huge grin on my face once my time was up.

The way I saw it, fifteen minutes back in anorexia's boot camp was a small price to pay for the guilt-free ecstasy that followed.

After watching me suffer with that guilt for so long, the staff must have agreed.

***

Now that I'd found the right mindset, my next job was dealing with the guilt lingering from the mindset I had before. It may have felt like I'd flicked some kind of switch that day at breakfast, but the brain changes incrementally, not all at once. After a year of my brain rewiring itself to make pain and sacrifice seem good and enjoyment seem bad, all the things that used to make me feel guilty still did. The only difference was, now I knew that guilt wasn't meant to be there, so most of the time, I could put up with it.

Sometimes, however, that guilt became a little too much, and when this happened, I had what my family and I came to know as a 'meltdown'. As hard as I tried to challenge every anorexic thought, there were times I simply didn't have the strength. An anorexic thought would stir for a little too long, the guilt would become unbearable, and within seconds, my mind would plunge into a terrifying darkness, completely consumed by the anorexic part of me. I'd grit my teeth and squeeze my eyes shut in protest, yet by that point, it was already too late: the bully was back in charge.

Meltdowns lasted anywhere between ten minutes and a few hours and usually happened just as I made some kind of breakthrough in my recovery. Anorexia hated losing control of my mind, and meltdowns were like its final, desperate attempts to drag me back to where I was before. Getting my independence back was key to getting my life back, yet the more the staff gave me, the more vulnerable to these meltdowns I became.

A week after I found 'the switch', the staff decided I was ready for my first night outside the Unit with family. By this stage, Mum and Dad were making the trip down to Wellington in turns, so the first weekend, I stayed in a motel with Dad, and the second, I stayed in one with Mum. I'd been too embarrassed to tell them about my time back on bed rest, so neither knew how much drama had unfolded that week. It wasn't until I wrote the previous chapter that they learned the full story and realised how lucky I was to leave the Unit with them so soon.

The weather during the first weekend was far from flash, so after checking into our motel, Dad and I headed off to the movies. We stopped in a few shops along the way, and in one of them, there was a jacket Dad could tell I liked the look of. I knew it was expensive and didn't like asking for things, but in the end, I didn't need to.

Dad told me how proud he was to see me getting better and bought it as recognition for how far I'd come. After so long of feeling like I was letting him down, hearing him say that meant the world. The way I saw it, getting the jacket was just a bonus.

Looking back, having such a good morning with Dad was probably what caused me to have such a bad afternoon. As I said, my brain was still wired to make me feel guilty for enjoying myself, so after such a positive start to the day, it was only a matter of time before that guilt became unbearable. I was trying so hard to feel happy, yet as soon as I did, I also felt like I didn't deserve it.

I can't remember what movie we saw that day, but considering how long I watched it, that's hardly surprising. As soon as we took our seats, my head dropped into my hands, and once the movie started, anorexia had launched what felt like a full-scale attack on my conscience.

A familiar darkness swept over me, suffocating my thoughts and swallowing any positive feelings whole. It was like teleporting straight into hell, yet anorexia was the devil, and guilt was the pitchfork it used to torture. I was paying the price for all the disobedience I'd been showing. In other words, I was paying the price for all the progress that I'd made.

Dad did all he could to snap me out of it, but nothing he said could pierce through the heavy darkness that held me. It was over a week since anorexia last had me under its control, so it was salvaging every moment and making up for all it had missed out on.

For as long as the meltdown lasted, I felt entirely at its mercy, yet eventually – whether my brain ran out of guilt or I finally found a way to dismantle it – the darkness cleared, and with that, a wave of relief washed over me. The meltdown was over, and I was left feeling like I'd been hit by a bus.

The weather was better the following weekend, so Mum and I stayed in a motel at the beach. We'd just got back from a walk when – in a remarkably similar fashion to the week before – the familiar darkness returned, and another meltdown began. Mum ended up hating meltdowns more than anyone, and I think the poem she wrote that day sums up brilliantly what they must have been like for her.

I watch you sitting, calm and clear

and then the shadow appears over you

and I know it's back

your eyes glaze over

you touch the side of your head

and you are no longer with me

it has come to claim you

my heart tightens in knots

I am so sad

our precious time together

is lost for a while

sometimes it's over in a moment

and you return to me

other times it claims you for hours

I hate it

I hate it with such intensity

how dare it steal my kind, innocent boy

sometimes you pound your head with your fist

that makes me so angry

and I want to shout at it

and tell it to leave you alone

to leave us all alone

let us all get on with our lives

what lies is it spinning to you now?

what promises does it make that could possibly appeal to you more than what we can offer you?

and then you come back

your eyes become clear

you don't look so pained and your face relaxes

and my heart lifts

and for now I am happy

***

After making it through two weekends outside the Unit, the staff agreed that I was ready for my first trip home. It may have required some persuasion, and my parents may have underplayed how serious those meltdowns were, but I think the right call was made. Even if I wasn't quite ready to go home, I was determined to convince everyone I was. In the end, that was enough.

I hadn't been home for almost four months, so it felt surreal to be back. Everything was just as I remembered it, yet at the same time, everything about it had changed. What were once pull-up bars were now just beams; what were once hill sprints were now just stairs; what were once vertical jump tests were now just ceilings. Everything still looked the same, yet my relationship with the space had completely changed. Before, it was a gym. Now, it was a home.

Mum and Dad knew that I needed to be kept busy, so although I spent most of the weekend at home, there was rarely a dull moment. I threw balls around with my brothers, went for short walks with Mum, watched TV with Dad, and whenever someone caught me staring off into space, they encouraged me to do something else. My family were as desperate as me for the weekend to go well, so the whole time I was back, one of them was there by my side.

As admirable as their efforts were, the guilt still managed to find a way through, and on each of the three days I was home, it eventually reached its breaking point. Mum and Dad were familiar with meltdowns by this stage, so aside from being there with me, they knew there wasn't much they could say or do to help. They would've gone through them for me if they could, but unfortunately, meltdowns were storms only I could weather. It was a case of just waiting for those storms to pass, and once they did, holding off the next one for as long as we could.

Beth Averill (Mum)

I must admit, I was nervous about having Harry home for the weekend. He'd experienced so much anorexia-inflicted trauma there the year before, and we didn't know how he'd respond to being back.

We tried to keep him busy the whole weekend, but there were periods each day when it all got too much for him. I remember sitting next to him for hours, trying to say the right things and react the right way when things weren't going well.

He was clearly fighting so hard to make things work, but it was exhausting for all of us. It was a relief to finally have him home, but I wondered how we'd cope when he eventually came back for good.

***

Having a taste of normal life only made me want it more, so when I returned to the Unit, I had my sights set on getting discharged as soon as possible. I felt like hospital had done all it could for me by that point, and as tough as I knew things would be on the outside, I was itching to begin the next stage of my recovery. A return to normal was now the only future I accepted, so the way I saw it, the sooner I took that next step, the better.

It was around this time that I started writing a daily journal. A great aunt sent it to me in the post, and although I was initially reluctant, I soon realised the benefits of getting things down on paper. It allowed me to make sense of what I was feeling, and as time went on, looking back on what I'd written became a great reminder of how far I'd come.

Even nine years on, some entries still make seriously tough reading. If I'm being honest, a lot of them I'll never share with anyone, let alone put in a book. They are as real, raw, and confronting as mental illness gets, yet at the same time, the fourteen-year-old version of me tells this story in a way the twenty-two-year-old version never could. For that reason, there are some entries I think are worth sharing.

04/02/2014 – Just finished my fifteen-minutes of basketball so my hands are really shaky from all the drugs. Now I'm sitting on the couch feeling like crap. I feel guilty about pretty much everything. Sometimes I worry that I'll never be normal again – that I'm just kidding myself to think I can get there. I know it's only anorexia making me feel this way, but that doesn't make it any less shit to deal with. I need to just keep telling myself that I deserve to enjoy life and be happy again and that one day this will all be over. I'm trying so hard to believe it.

11/02/2014 – Average day today. Started off with school but the doctor pulled me out to have a talk. He said that if I keep going the way I am, I could be discharged as early as next week. This is really exciting, but it's hard not to worry about the challenges I've still got ahead of me. At the moment I feel ready for home food-wise but not exercise and depression-wise. I know I've just got to stay positive about it so I don't have another meltdown – the last thing I want is for the doctors to change their minds.

19/02/2014 – Started off the day by getting weighed. Was the same as yesterday and am still above my target weight which is good. Had school this morning but couldn't get anything done again. My mind is still all over the place. Found out I'm getting discharged tomorrow at 2:30pm. I'm sort of excited but mainly overwhelmed by it all. I just hope life outside of here is better than it was before. If it goes bad then I guess I'll just have to fake it till I make it, but hopefully it all goes well so I can catch up in school and become happy again. That's all I want.

20/02/2014 – Finally I'm home. Today kind of felt like the first day of the rest of my life. It's a bit like I'm starting my life from scratch again. I didn't go to school at the Unit this morning because I had to pack my bags for home. Then I had my Poroporoaki (a Māori farewell) which was pretty emotional. I was amazed by what everyone said in their speeches and in the card they gave me. Then I got taken to the airport. After my flight was delayed a couple of times, I got onto the plane and sat next to a nice old lady who chewed my ear off. Once I got home I had a big meltdown and now I'm feeling like I want to die. I just hope tomorrow is better – I don't know what I'll do if it's not.

Tucking into some cheese as a little fella.

Posing with our very tolerant cat.

About to head off for my first day at Gisborne Central School.

With my brothers, Jack (left) and Oscar, enjoying a feed of fish and chips.

With Jack (right) and Oscar during a family holiday. I'm about nine at this point.

Like pigs in shit. That's me showing off in the middle.

Taken after my last game of rugby in 2012, about four months before I started high school.

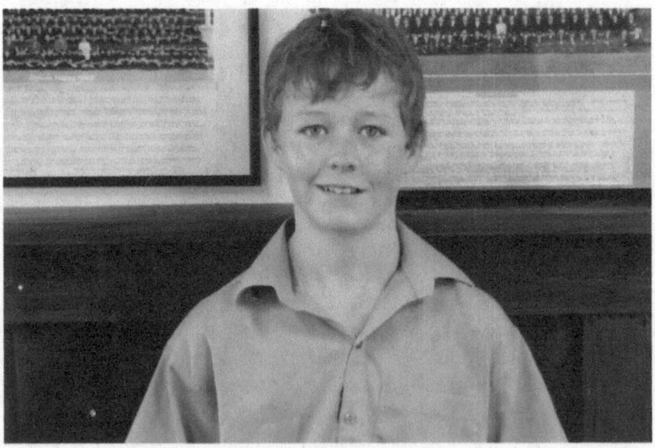

In the hostel dining hall before my first day at Napier Boys'.

After finishing my leg of the Triple Peaks, a few weeks after starting at Napier Boys'.

With Oscar (left), Dad, Mum and Jack (right) in Tauranga, the day before I woke up into what felt like a nightmare.

Running in the school road race a few months later. I'm about as happy and healthy as I look.

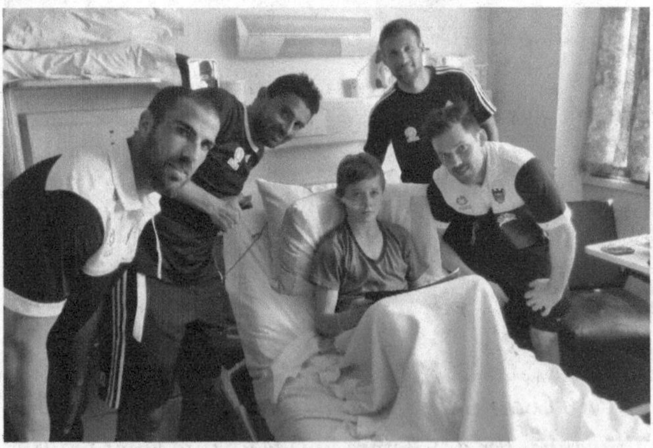

Being visited by some Wellington Phoenix players near the end of my stint at Hastings Hospital. I doubt I was offering much chat in return.

Fourteen

HOME

IF 2013 WAS THE worst year of my life, then 2014 will always be the year I achieved the most. It may not have felt like a success at the time – in fact, I spent most of that year feeling like a failure – but given where I was in January, getting to where I was in December was a triumph against all odds. For as long as I live, I'll remain grateful for the determination and resilience of the 2014 version of me.

Now that I'd left the Unit, the CAFS team took back responsibility for the medical side of my care. I had the same psychiatrist, psychologist, and dietitian as I did in Hastings Hospital, and we met once a week for what they called 'family therapy'. I never looked forward to these sessions, and I hated that my family were dragged into them with me, but looking back, they did serve an important purpose. The CAFS team were the final link between hospital and normal life, and as I transitioned from one back into the other, they made sure it happened at the right pace.

They wanted me to ease back into normal life slowly, so I spent my first two weeks outside the Unit at home with family. Mum and Dad took as much time off work as they could, and whenever they weren't there, a pair of grandparents always were. My family may have lacked the expertise of the staff back at the Unit, but when it came to my recovery, they helped in a way that only family can. Without their continued love and support, I wouldn't have lived to see the end of 2014, let alone made it the success it was.

Each family therapy session began with me getting weighed. Now that I'd reached my 'target' weight, my next goal was to reach what they called my 'ideal' weight. I was still a long way off this when I first got home, so my food intake had to ramp up even further. Thankfully, eating was nowhere near the drama it used to be. Each mouthful still went down like a shot of liquid guilt, but that feeling lost its intensity with time. As tough as it was to get it down, I knew it was doing wonders for my recovery.

I may have had a better handle on eating, but when it came to exercise, anorexia was still very much in control. Now that I was home, it would have been quite easy to slip in workouts when my family wasn't looking. This made me feel guiltier for sitting down like I was meant to because, unlike in the Unit, now I felt like I had a choice. For the first week I was back, hardly a minute went by where I didn't at least toy with the idea of burning some extra energy, and although I only gave in to these urges a few times, they consumed me all the same.

To make things easier, the CAFS team let me start exercising for thirty minutes a day instead of just fifteen. I usually spent this time running as far as I could in fifteen minutes before turning around and running home. As you'd expect, this did a great job of relieving some of that guilt, but thirty minutes is a long time to push your body to its limits. I'd feel great at the end of each run, but then I'd spend the rest of each day worrying about the next. I'd only been home a few days, yet I already felt anorexia clawing its way back into control.

Luckily, I was no longer the same kid I was a month ago. Instead of accepting that situation – or letting it get worse – I realised I had the power to make it better. Allowing each day to revolve around thirty minutes of exercise clearly wasn't making me happy, so I knew that my relationship with exercise would have to change.

Everyone knows that exercise is good for your health, but I didn't want to do it because I felt like I had to. If I was going to exercise, I wanted to do it because I enjoyed it. After all, if I didn't enjoy it and it wasn't making me happier, what value was it really adding? If it was going to be part of my life, it, first of all, had to satisfy that criterion.

I knew the only way I'd start enjoying exercise was if I dropped the intensity, and the only way I'd do that was if I stopped measuring it. Anorexia thrives on comparing one day's performance to the next, so to prevent this from happening, I started running without a watch. Being in the running team had made me an expert at working out 'minutes per kilometre', yet by taking off my watch, I was telling myself once and for all that I didn't care how fast I ran.

Instead, I tried to focus on enjoyment. I worked out how far I could go in thirty minutes if I ran at a more enjoyable pace (for me, this was just more than a jog), found a few routes that covered this distance, and ran only one of these routes each day. This meant I went the same distance no matter how fast I ran, so by pushing myself, all I was doing was making my exercise session shorter. If I wanted to run for the whole half hour, I had to learn how to stick to a more enjoyable pace.

Luckily, switching to this new approach worked a treat. It took me a few days to bring the intensity down, and running slower did leave me with extra guilt when I finished, but after a week, just covering that distance each day felt like enough.

I was still a long way off enjoying exercise – after all, it's hard to have fun when every second thought is screaming at you to go faster – but I knew it was only a matter of time before I did. A return to normal was the only future I believed in, so the way I saw it, any problems I faced now were temporary. For that reason alone, I was willing to push through them.

***

I'd been home for a week when a teacher from the Regional Health School visited me. New Zealand has three of these schools, each providing teachers for students whose health prevents them from attending school full-time. Luckily for me, the teacher for my region was Michelle, who just happened to be an absolute legend.

For the next few months, Michelle spent two hours a week helping me catch up to my classmates back at Napier Boys'. Concentration was still a huge issue, but Michelle had a real knack for keeping me on task. There were gaps in my knowledge that would take the next few years to fill, but by helping me work through some of the assessments I'd missed, Michelle made sure it never looked too bad on paper. The beauty of it was, she managed all of this without ever stressing me out.

After having a few sessions with Michelle, I started attending the odd class back at Napier Boys'. I may have been a boarder the year before, but the CAFS team made it clear that a return to the hostel wouldn't be happening for at least another year, if at all. Luckily, living only twenty minutes away meant I could switch to being a day boy.

My parents worked full-time, but having both sets of grand-parents nearby meant I could be at school only for as long as I could handle each day. This gave me all the flexibility I needed as I transitioned back to full-time school and meant an emergency pick-up was only ever a phone call and twenty minutes away.

Still, the decision to return to Napier Boys' was a tough one, and if I'm being honest, I seriously considered going elsewhere. I knew I could do with a fresh start, and now that I couldn't board, going to a school closer to home would have made things a lot easier for my family.

Besides, after my time at Napier Boys' the year before, even thinking about going back was enough to send a shiver down my spine. I'd had some of the darkest days of my life at that place, and after months of embarrassment the year before, I worried how the other boys would treat me when I returned. Would they remember all my weird exercise routines? Would they still treat me like I was some kind of freak? Would they notice how different I looked and how much slower I was at running?

In the end, I decided to return to Napier Boys' for two reasons. For one, I didn't want anorexia dictating my life more than it had already. I knew I'd have never left Napier Boys' if it wasn't for anorexia, so as tough as it was to go back, I was determined to make it work. Going to that school may have been a big part of the reason I developed anorexia in the first place, but the way I saw it, no one was to blame for what I'd been through but anorexia itself. If I was going to switch schools, I certainly didn't want anorexia playing a part in my decision.

The second – and more significant – reason I decided to stay at Napier Boys' was a man named Rob Silver. Rob is the school's counsellor, and aside from being great at his job, he is easily the kindest and most selfless human I've met. I didn't have the awareness or balls to ask him for help the year before, but if I had, I know things would have never turned out the way they did. He saves lives each day he goes to work, and behind my family, he'd have more influence on my recovery than anyone else.

As I integrated back into full-time school, Rob's office became my safe space. He made it clear that I could go there whenever I was struggling to cope and that he'd do all he could to help no matter how busy he was. Whether that was making the time for a quick chat, a long chat, giving me his office to study in or giving me a ride home, Rob always went the extra mile to make my life easier. High school can be intimidating at the best of times, but when battling a mental illness, even walking through the front gates can seem impossible. Thanks to Rob, I knew there was always a place for me to go.

As a counsellor at an all-boys school, Rob admits he didn't have much experience dealing with anorexia before me. Well, if that was the case, he certainly didn't show it. What he may have lacked in experience, he made up for with his empathy and willingness to learn, and by the end of that year, Rob probably knew as much about anorexia as I knew myself.

He asked all the right questions and responded to my answers in all the right ways, yet his patience on days when I didn't reply meant the most. Whether I was having a meltdown or just didn't feel like talking, Rob spent just as many hours counselling as he did waiting patiently for me to lift my head out of my hands. His office was the one place at school where I could stop pretending I was okay, and as much of an inconvenience as this must have been for him, he never once made it known to me.

None of it would have been possible without him – it's as simple as that.

<u>06/03/2014</u> – *Woke up feeling crap so went for my half-hour run. Made me feel better but still feel guilty for running slow. Then went to Gran and Grandad's for a bit before Mum took me to school for the first time. Was quite nervous and felt sick but also a bit excited. Mr Silver (Rob) organised a couple of mates from class to meet me in his office and go with me to form class. Was pretty overwhelming but managed to get through it without having a meltdown. Then went to interval and caught up with some hostel mates before going home again. Everyone was really nice but I felt guilty to be back – it feels like anorexia just wants me in hospital again.*

13/03/2014 – Achieved a lot today. Went to Granny and Papa's and then they took me to school. Felt pretty crap in the car but once I got there I was alright and managed to get through interval and a period of science. I'm so far behind I feel like I'll never catch up. Just wish I could enjoy life like I used to – at the moment each day feels like a chore.

17/03/2014 – Had an alright day today. Went for a run and didn't feel like I had to push myself. After that Michelle came around and we finished my first science assessment. Then Mum took me over to school. I got through my science and English periods again. At lunch a lot of boys asked me questions about where I'd been and what had happened to me but I think I handled it okay. Just told them I had problems with my heart from doing too much running last year – that seemed to do the trick.

31/03/2014 – Today was pretty rough. I was planning to go to school for three periods but could only handle one and had a massive meltdown in Mr Silver's office. In the end Mum had to rescue me and drop me off at Granny and Papa's so she could go back to work.

Feeling really depressed this week for some reason, but the anorexic stuff is definitely getting better.

<u>*04/04/2014*</u> *– Achieved heaps today. Had my first day going to four out of five periods at school. I was really struggling to start with but managed to hold off the meltdown. Gran picked me up after lunch and then I went for a run. Had lots of thoughts telling me that I wasn't pushing myself hard enough so ended up going as hard as I could for a few minutes. First time that's happened in a while. Can't let it happen again.*

***

I'd only been home for three months, yet by the end of Term One, I was already attending school for a few hours each day. Some days were much easier than others, and I was still spending about as much time in Rob's office as I was in a classroom, but even getting that far surpassed all expectations. The CAFS team had set me the goal of attending school full-time by the end of the year, so to be that close by April was a great start.

During the first school holidays, Mum and I flew to Auckland for a night. There was a counsellor up there with lots of experience dealing with eating disorders, and Mum, being as desperate as she was for me to get better, booked me an appointment to see her.

We weren't getting much out of the family therapy sessions with the CAFS team, and as great as Rob was, I didn't want to keep relying on missed classes or lunchtimes to get the help I needed going forward. Rob would have happily seen me outside of school if he knew this was a concern, but I didn't want to take any more time from the man who'd already given me so much.

After only five minutes with the counsellor in Auckland, I could tell I'd struck gold. Whether it was all her experience treating eating disorders or just the person she was, she and I seemed to 'click' in a way that made me feel so understood. She described the bully between my ears as if she'd met it several times before, and when I explained my thoughts and feelings to her, she responded as if it all made perfect sense. For the first time, I felt like someone genuinely 'got me' and what was going on inside my head.

It's yet another example of how lucky I was. Life may not have dealt me a very good hand in the past year, but adding Rob and the private counsellor to my already stacked support team was like winning the mental illness lottery.

A lot of people don't get the chance to see the mental health professionals they need, let alone the ones that could help them the most. They might live in an area where the sector is understaffed and the waitlists are far too long; they might have a family to support and feel like they don't have the time; they might have the time but not the money, so they're forced settle with someone who doesn't help or risk going broke trying to find someone who can; or, perhaps worst of all, their minds might fool them into thinking they're a hopeless case that can't be saved. Recovering from mental illness was the hardest thing I've ever had to do, but again, compared to most who face that challenge, I had it pretty damn good.

The trip up to Auckland would be the only time I'd see the counsellor in person. From then on, we met once a week via Skype. These sessions usually happened on a Friday after school, and although they were often the last thing I felt like doing, I could tell how much they helped.

Each session enabled me to become more aware of my thought patterns, where they were going wrong, and, importantly, how to stop them in their tracks when they did. This made the anorexic thoughts less frequent, and when they did occur, much easier for me to pick apart. Having the motivation to beat anorexia hadn't been an issue, but now I was getting all the tools I needed to make it happen.

A year earlier, I was on the slippery slope, and anorexia was the one gaining all the control within my mind. Now the roles had been reversed, but unlike anorexia, I wasn't going to stop until the job was done. I wasn't going to stop until my mind was mine alone, and anorexia – the co-inhabitant of that mind – was dead.

Fifteen

FAKE IT TILL YOU MAKE IT

It only took two weeks for me to work up to a few hours of school each day, but making the leap to full-time school wasn't quite so easy. After four months in hospital without any pressure to 'fit in' socially, navigating the dynamics of high school life was exhausting.

If I could have sat in a class by myself all day, I would have managed, but that's not quite how high school works. Unless I was in Rob's office, I felt a constant pressure to be 'normal', and for me, that meant pretending everything was okay when most of the time, it wasn't. When all you want to do is crawl into a ball and cry, six hours is a long time to act happy.

Even with the help I was getting from Rob and the counsellor in Auckland, a month after the Term One holidays, I still hadn't had my first full day at school. Whether it was sitting down for long periods, cracking jokes with mates or sharing food from the canteen, being at school meant there was no escaping the kind of pleasures anorexia told me I didn't deserve.

Everything I had to do to be 'normal' made me feel guilty, and I could only hide behind a smile for so long. The guilt eventually broke through the disguise, and when that happened – usually after three or four hours – school was the last place I wanted to be.

Around this time, Rob raised the idea of me spending time at Community High, a small co-ed school around the corner from Napier Boys'. It's a short-term alternative for students unable to attend one of the local high schools, with two teachers and only a dozen students. Although most students are there for disciplinary issues, in recent years, a growing number have been those battling a mental illness. Instead of going home when I couldn't cope at Napier Boys', Rob suggested I start going there.

At first, I was adamant that it wouldn't be happening. From what I'd heard, the only kids at Community High were those who'd been expelled from their other schools. It certainly didn't seem like a place for well-behaved kids like me having problems with their mental health. As far as I could tell, all going there would do was take me further from the life I was trying to get back.

It wasn't until Rob showed me around the place that I changed my mind. As I walked around the classroom and talked to the other students, I couldn't help but notice how much we all had in common. Their reasons for not attending school may not seem as innocent as mine, but our lives had all come to similar crossroads; either we changed the way we lived them, or we'd continue being outcasts in a world that wouldn't change for us. The demons I had to fight were different to theirs, but at the end of the day, we were all struggling to exist within the same world. I was no better than them, and they were no better than me. We were all just trying to sort our shit out, and Community High was there to help.

22/05/2014 – Today was hard but feel like I achieved a lot. Woke up feeling motivated and went over to Community High for the first time. Didn't want to go but Mr Silver told me to at least check it out. The teachers were both really nice and I even got along well with the other kids there. Really put things in perspective for me – they might seem like bad kids, but I need to change just as much as they do. Went to three periods at NBHS then had rugby training after school. Really enjoyed it.

From that day on, I was taken to Community High first thing each morning and picked up whenever school or rugby practice finished in the afternoon. There was the odd day where I didn't make it out of the car, but not a day went by where I didn't at least put my uniform on and make the trip over. This allowed me to get into a daily routine and, with time, made the trip to school seem a lot less daunting.

Rugby season was in full swing by this stage, so there were also two days a week where I stayed for training after school. I wasn't meant to play any competitive sport that year, but the CAFS team agreed to let me play rugby if I stayed in the lightest (least competitive) weight grade.

As gutted as I was to hear I couldn't trial for a better team, I could understand where they were coming from. If there was one thing I'd learned in the past year, it was that competitive sport and I don't go well together. I also knew that another season in the lightest weight grade would have its perks. I was already ten kilos heavier than I was the year before, so unlike last season, now

I'd be one of the heaviest players on the field. This made rugby a completely different ball game and, as the women in my family found out, one that was a lot easier to watch.

During my days at Community High, I usually just did what the other students were doing – or at least, I did what they were meant to be doing. Whether catching up on schoolwork or doing group activities, I made it a goal to participate fully no matter how grim my state of mind.

This helped me build the mental stamina I needed for full-time school, and I soon found myself pushing through what would have previously been meltdown-worthy levels of guilt. I started getting my confidence back, and although the other students weren't my usual choice of company, within a week, I was getting along with some of them like best mates. They may not have been very diligent when it came to schoolwork, but when it came to taking life less seriously, they were just the role models I needed.

Whenever I felt ready, I'd walk around the corner to Napier Boys'. Some days I'd only stay for a class or two before returning, but as the weeks went by, these stints got longer and longer. I was usually on the verge of a meltdown by the time I got back to Community High, so the next challenge was pulling myself together as soon as possible before plucking up the courage to try again. There were plenty of days where I didn't make it back to Napier Boys', and plenty more where I didn't leave Community High in the first place, but spending full days between them was still an almighty step forward.

I was still a long way off feeling happy, but the more time I spent at school, the better I got at pretending I was. 'Fake it till you make it' and 'one day at a time' became my mantras, and I tried to maintain what felt like excessive optimism towards my future. No matter how miserable I felt, I convinced myself that happiness was only just around the corner and that once I got there, life would be better than I could even imagine.

All I had to do was stay in the fight, and one day soon, the fighting would be able to stop.

<u>27/05/2014</u> – *Really good day today. Woke up feeling crap but was determined to make things better. Went to school for three periods then walked back to Community High when the guilt got too much. Had rugby after school – felt good to have so much energy again. Also good to have hands that aren't numb and work properly. Made me want to keep putting on weight so I can get stronger and play*

even better – first time I've said something like that in a while! After dinner I made myself a hot chocolate which was a huge thing for me.

<u>*04/06/2014*</u> *– Shit day today, probably the worst in a while. Mum took me to Community High but I wasn't able to go in so she took me home. Had a meltdown for most of the day – felt like I was trapped back in that nightmare. Didn't go to rugby training which I feel shit about now. I'm trying so hard to make things better but just wish I could make it happen faster. Need to just stay focused on getting through one day at a time – that way it doesn't feel impossible.*

<u>*10/06/2014*</u> *– Achieved heaps today. Had my first full day at NBHS which I'm really proud of. Was struggling heaps at the start but found a way to push through. Felt like I was on a roll so after school I decided not to do any exercise even though I'm allowed to do half an hour. Managed to fight off the guilt for a few hours but have just had a pretty major meltdown. I'm so sick of feeling guilty even though I know I'm doing nothing wrong. It feels like anorexia is punishing me for getting my life back.*

<u>*17/06/2014*</u> *– Tough day today but found a way to get through*

it. Woke up feeling crap but convinced myself to get up and keep fighting. Have to keep believing that all this stuff is temporary and that I've got an awesome life waiting for me once I beat it. Went to NBHS for four periods then went back to Community High for a bit. Hopefully the last time I'll have to go back there. Still feeling way behind academically but slowly getting my concentration back which is good. Socially I'm doing alright but need to remember to just be myself and not worry too much about what other people think. Need to remember that all I need to do is get happy – everything else is irrelevant. After school Mum picked me up to go to the psychiatrist at CAFS. That went really well and he decided to reduce my meds again.

<u>*18/06/2014*</u> *– Going to stop writing this stuff down because I don't think it's helping anymore.*

***

Thankfully, the second half of 2014 was nowhere near as tough as the first. By mid-June, I was back at Napier Boys' full-time, and by July, the CAFS team had officially discharged me. The psychiatrist still had to monitor any changes to my medication, but aside from that, all I had was a weekly Skype session with the counsellor in Auckland and the odd catch-up with Rob at school. I was now several steps closer to a life free of mental illness, and as had been the case all year, that made me want to beat it even more.

Now that I was back at school full-time, my next goal was to join my mates back at the hostel. This may seem outrageous considering I was only four months out of a psych ward, but after making all the progress I had since then, I saw almost no limits to what I could achieve. The way I saw it, the more time I could spend 'faking it' each day, the closer I'd get to 'making it', so boarding school would be a great way to speed up the process.

The CAFS team told my parents I wouldn't be ready to board until at least the following year, but like so many times before, I was determined to prove them and their predictions about me wrong. Not only was I going to be boarding by the end of the year – I was going to be boarding by the end of the term.

It took me a while to convince my parents, Rob, and the counsellor in Auckland that I was ready, but they eventually agreed to let me stay in the hostel on the last night of Term Two. There was a social on that night with Napier Girls', so I was able to convince them that logistically, it made sense to just pick me up after school the following day. My parents, especially Mum, were hesitant to let me go back so soon, but in the end, they trusted I knew my limits better than they did.

Beth Averill (Mum)

I didn't think I'd ever let Harry return to the hostel. It was the place he developed anorexia the year before, and I worried how he'd cope if the wheels ever fell off in that environment.

Harry and I could have fairly open conversations about how he was feeling by this point, so I had to just trust that if Harry told me he would be okay, he would be okay. I had to believe that he knew his boundaries better than me, so contrary to the advice of the CAFS team and his counsellor, we decided to let him stay a night.

I felt so proud when I picked him up the following afternoon. No one would have had any idea how much strength he showed by keeping a brave face for that long. No one would have had any idea how miraculous it was for him to be back there, let alone so soon.

At the start of Term Three, the plan was for me to ease into weekly boarding the same way I'd eased back into school. I'd start by aiming for just one night a week, and from there, I'd transition to four nights a week at a pace I felt comfortable with. The decision to stay would always be made on a night-by-night basis, and no matter what the time of day, an emergency pick-up would only ever be a phone call and twenty minutes away. I'd meet with the hostel matron each night to take my medication, and my older brother, Jack, would check in with me as often as he could. Having these safety nets in place eased my parent's worries, and although I was never too worried myself, it was nice to know that help was there if I needed it.

As with every other milestone that year, the transition to weekly boarding happened much faster than expected. I had my first four-night stay in the hostel just three weeks into Term Three, and a couple of months later, I was staying from Monday to Friday consistently.

There were plenty of days where I felt like I was 'faking it' for its entirety, but the more of these days I got under my belt, the less frequent they became. It felt great to be back living with mates, and now that I didn't have a fourteen-hour exercise regime to stick to, boarding school was a completely different ball game to the year before.

Whether going to the dairy, playing social sport, or just sitting around talking the kind of rubbish teenage boys do, all the fun that used to be off-limits suddenly became part of my day-to-day life. I was finally able to spend my days the way my mates were spending theirs, and although I did most of it with a cloud of guilt hanging over me, I soon found myself having moments of genuine enjoyment.

No one ever mentioned how weird I was the year before, and there were never too many questions about where I'd been over summer. This surprised me, but I soon learned that when it comes to teenage boys, all anyone really cares about is what's happening in the here and now. As far as they were concerned, all that mattered was the person I'd become, how fun I was to be around, and how I treated them in return. That may not be how it works at every school or hostel, but with one bully already stirring the pot between my ears, I was grateful it worked that way at mine.

With each month, the emergency pick-ups got fewer and further between, and as I moved into the final term of 2014, the progress kept coming. My teachers tried not to put too much pressure on me that year, so they told me I didn't have to sit any end-of-year exams if I didn't want to. As long as I felt I had a good grip on the content, they'd allow me to come back in 2015 as a Year Eleven, no different (on paper) to anyone else my age.

This was reassuring, but I decided to sit the exams anyway. Knowing there wasn't pressure to pass made it seem like something I could handle, and having missed two sets of exams already, I knew I could do with the extra practice before becoming a senior.

I put more pressure on myself than I should have, but in the end, I managed to get through the exams without my mental health taking too much of a hit. There's a fine line between doing your best and handicapping yourself by trying too hard, and finding that 'happy' medium would take me another few years to master. I was just stoked to have given the exams a go, and after everything I'd been through, to have made it through my first two years of high school alive.

***

I didn't need any extra motivation to get better, but when my Gran passed away at the end of that year, I got it anyway. Alongside my parents, brothers, and other three grandparents, Gran was a vital piece of my recovery puzzle.

She spent hours doing pick-ups and drop-offs, days looking after me when I couldn't go to school and played countless rounds of golf with me to help pass the time. Yet as amazing a grandparent as she was, as with my Granny, Papa, and Grandad, she was an even better role model for a life well lived. She would have done anything to see me happy again, and for as long as I live, I'll regret that I didn't give her the chance. I know it wasn't my fault she died, but I felt a lot of guilt for making the end of her life as stressful as it was.

The last time I saw Gran, I thanked her for all her support, apologised for causing her so much worry and promised her that no matter what happened, I would never stop trying to be happier. I'd made a few promises that year, but this is a promise I've thought about most days since.

I'll always be gutted that Gran didn't see me recover completely, but ever since she passed, I've made it a goal to live my life in a way that would have made her proud – not through any kind of material success, but by becoming the happiest person I can. It's an ambitious goal that I'll probably never achieve, but that's the very beauty of it – I'll be chasing it for the rest of my life.

To the outsider, my life now looked much like it would have if anorexia had never entered the picture. I was a weekly boarder at Napier Boys', I'd passed my Year Ten exams, I played only the sports I loved, I was the same height and weight as most boys my age, I had a good group of mates, great physical health, and without looking too closely, I appeared to have great mental health, too.

My recovery was still far from finished, but as far as most people could tell, I'd got my life back. All I had to do now was start enjoying it.

Sixteen

THE COMEBACK

COMPARED TO 2014, THE next two years were a picnic. I'd already learned how to eat, how to exercise without torturing myself, and in general, how to behave less like an anorexic and more like a normal teenager.

To beat anorexia completely, now all I had to do was push those behaviours further and, if possible, eliminate the guilt that came with them. That meant eating more, exercising less, having more fun, and whenever necessary, reminding myself that it was happiness, not success, that was my priority. Guilt was the last thing between me and a life free of anorexia, and as 2014 rolled into 2015, I felt that life getting closer and closer.

From this point, the best way to measure my progress was the amount of guilt I felt, and the best way to measure that was the frequency of my meltdowns. Meltdowns only happened when the guilt became too much for me to bear, so having less of them was a clear sign that anorexia had less influence on my day-to-day life.

For the first half of 2015, I was holding off most meltdowns until I came home each weekend and only needed an emergency pickup about once a month. This was an improvement from the previous year, but when I had them, the meltdowns were still just as long and terrifying as ever. They still lasted hours, and in the midst of them, any progress I'd made became irrelevant – I was back in the torture chamber of my 2013 mind, utterly defenceless against the power-tripping bully back in charge.

By the second half of 2015, not only were my meltdowns less frequent, but I was pulling myself out of them a lot quicker. I only had them around once a month, and most of them weren't lasting any longer than an hour.

I'm not sure if less guilt was building up or if I was just dealing with it better, but shorter meltdowns were a welcomed relief for my family and me. I'd had hundreds of them by this point, but they were still just as horrible for everyone involved. Each one inevitably came to an end, but there was always that same fear that one of them wouldn't and that anorexia, the bully between my ears, would be back for good.

If there was a good thing about meltdowns, it was that when they finished, I was left hating anorexia even more than before. They were a small taste of the nightmare I used to live in and an instant reminder of how much I'd suffered at anorexia's hands. When the guilt lifted and my mind eventually cleared, I was left feeling grateful to have come as far as I had, furious at anorexia for what it did and continued to do to me, and more determined than ever to kick it to the curb.

Anger isn't usually a helpful emotion, but when it came to beating anorexia, it was one of the best tools I had.

***

When I started high school a couple of years earlier, I assumed the best part of life was over. As far as I could tell, that was when childhood ended and growing up began, and from what I'd heard, growing up wasn't anywhere near as fun. There were a few perks, like getting your driver's licence and getting closer to finishing school, but aside from that, it was pretty much all bad news.

I'd already learned a lot about life since 2013, yet the older I got, the more I realised how wrong I used to be about growing up. It does come with challenges that childhood doesn't, but as it turns out, these are far outweighed by its perks: you get more independence, you get treated with more respect, you can start going to parties, you can start earning money, you get smarter, taller, stronger, and in general, you start experiencing more of what the world has to offer.

It may feel like the stakes are higher and the outcomes of your decisions are more permanent, but when you're approaching life the right way, that only makes it more exciting. In fact, if my experience is anything to go by, growing up is just as, if not more fun as being a kid – the fun just comes in new, more age-appropriate forms.

The year before, I only socialised at school because I had to, not because it made me feel good. Aside from getting better at 'pretending' to be happy, I never felt like I was getting as much from the experience as those around me. To be honest, the whole thing felt like an act. There was the odd moment of enjoyment, but this was always followed by guilt, as if by having fun, I was somehow breaking the code of growing up

Now that the guilt was wearing off and I didn't need to 'fake it' so often, spending time with mates was fast becoming my favourite thing to do. Rather than just making me better at pretending to be happy, now it was making me happier directly. Interval and lunchtime regained their spots as weekday highlights, and if there was ever a party on at the weekend, not even anorexia's best efforts could prevent me from showing up and enjoying myself. I was becoming more comfortable in my own skin, more confident, and with time, more sure of myself and the man I was becoming.

None of my mates ever talked to me about what I'd been through, either because they didn't know, or for those who did, because they felt awkward that I hadn't raised it with them first. I wasn't necessarily embarrassed or ashamed to have had a mental illness, but as a guy, I did feel a lot of embarrassment and shame to have had anorexia. It felt like a dent in my masculinity, and by admitting the truth, I was worried I'd open myself up to questions I didn't yet know how to answer. Can guys get anorexia? Why didn't you just eat? Did you feel like you were fat, or did you just not like food? You don't look anorexic – does that mean you're over it now?

There were plenty of times I cancelled plans because I wasn't in the right headspace, but instead of telling the truth, I'd always lie and make up some other excuse. It was always a 'sorry, I've got a stomach bug' or 'sorry, I've got a family dinner' and never a 'sorry, the guilt from anorexia is really bad today' or 'sorry, I feel like I'm about to have a meltdown.'

I know my mates would have been supportive if I'd told them the truth, but for me, it always seemed easier to pretend everything in my head was okay again. I didn't want them to see me differently, and I was scared that if I admitted my vulnerability, they would start being more careful with what they said around me. That might sound like a good thing, but after so long feeling like I was abnormal, the last thing I wanted was more special treatment. If that meant being on the end of a few unintentionally triggering comments, so be it. I just wanted to feel like one of the boys again, so the way I saw it, the sooner I got over those anorexic insecurities, the better.

I know this wasn't the best strategy, and looking back, I wish I'd been more open with my mates about my struggles. Like most fifteen-year-olds, I guess I was too hung up on 'fitting in' to initiate the kinds of discussions that would have helped us all. It takes a lot of guts and maturity to be honest about these things, but if there's one thing I've learned in the years since, it's that nothing bad happens when you are.

The further I got into 2015, the more fun I started having, not just because my mental health was improving but because I was finally experiencing the perks of growing up. Yes, there was more pressure to do well at school, and the costs of failing at anything were higher than they used to be, but to my surprise, that didn't make my life any less fun or my mind any less happy.

You can only feel as much pressure as you put on yourself, and as time went on, I got better and better at taking that pressure off. Rather than worrying about long-term outcomes, I tried to think of every exam, sports game, or social situation as an opportunity to improve my state of mind. An exam wasn't something to feel threatened by, but a chance to get better at handling stress; keeping fit wasn't something to obsess over, but a reason to get outdoors and appreciate the bliss of a healthy mind; talking to 'popular' people wasn't something to feel anxious about, but a way to get better at talking, gain confidence, and figure out the kind of person I wanted to be.

All aspects of growing up that used to scare me became opportunities for self-improvement. Yet, by basing my goals around happiness instead of success, I soon found myself performing better than ever. My grades improved, I started playing better sport, and my social life continued going from strength to strength.

Contrary to what I used to believe, I was learning that happiness wasn't something I had to sacrifice to be successful. If anything, it was becoming the most vital ingredient and maintaining it was like unlocking some kind of superpower. The older I got, the happier I felt and, as if by accident, the more I was able to achieve.

This debunked everything I used to believe about success, happiness, and the relationship between the two. Yet again, I was proving anorexia to be completely full of shit.

***

By 2016, the once debilitating guilt was nothing more than a proverbial sniffle in the nose, and meltdowns were so rare that when they did happen, they felt like blasts from my anorexic past.

I'd gone from taking three medications a day to one, my counselling sessions had shifted from weekly to monthly, and when it came to my schoolwork, sport and social life, things were better than they'd ever been before. I was now on the very cusp of beating anorexia, and already I could sniff the magic of a post-anorexic life.

A few months into that year, I met with a psychiatrist about changing my medication. I'd been on the same anti-depressant since arriving in hospital in 2013, and although it kept a smile on my dial, there were some annoying side effects that I was keen to start living without. Keeping my mood in check was one thing, but if another drug could do the same without the inconveniences, why not try it out?

Like the counsellor in Auckland, the new psychiatrist seemed to 'get me' from the moment we met. He said that finding the right anti-depressant was like finding the right pair of shoes: the ones you try on first may not be the best fit, so if you're not satisfied with how they feel, it's probably worth trying on another pair. Building on what I'd learned in science class, he then explained how anti-depressants worked, and from there, suggested why another drug might be better than the one I was on.

I've always been intellectually curious, so hearing this was like music to my ears. I loved that he seemed to know his stuff, but I loved even more that he took the time to explain it to me. It made the decision to switch drugs seem easy, and although I'd have preferred to be on nothing at all, he assured me that taking medication was nothing to be ashamed of. Like diabetics taking insulin to correct their blood sugar levels, some people's brains need an artificial boost to correct their mood. It doesn't mean you're inferior or any less tough – it's just science, and if part of the solution to your problem has been found, you might as well let it help you.

Within a couple of months, it was clear that the new drug was working a treat. The side effects of the previous one had all but disappeared, I was feeling more like myself than I had in years, and my recovery had taken another almighty leap in the right direction. Clearly, it was worth trying on another pair of shoes.

With everything going so well, I decided to finish up with the counsellor in Auckland. I'd been having the Skype sessions for over two years, and although they were now only happening once a month, they rarely lasted the whole hour like they used to. There just wasn't enough for us to talk about, and I often felt like I was sharing my thoughts and feelings with her for the sake of it.

She had helped me develop all the strategies I needed to beat anorexia, so aside from reminding me how far I'd come, there just wasn't anything left for her to do. Besides, the sessions were always on a Friday afternoon, so they were also becoming a serious hindrance to my social life.

The counsellor made it clear that I could see her again if I needed to, but at the end of our last session, I was almost certain it wouldn't be necessary. Only I could deal anorexia its final blows, and thanks to her, I now felt more than capable of finishing the job on my own. I had the right mindset screwed in place, a toolbox full of all the tools I'd need to keep it there, and an almost obsessive drive to become the happiest person I could be.

In other words, my mind had already become anorexia's worst nightmare, and if it wasn't already, that bully between my ears would very soon be dead.

Seventeen

PULLING THE FINGER

IF THE BULLY I came to know as anorexia was plucked from deep within my brain and plonked on the floor in front of me, what would I do? Would I force it to exercise without eating until its heart stopped beating? Would I shower it with insults and lies until it hated itself? Would I spare it from the suffering it caused me by killing it on the spot? Or alternatively, would I express forgiveness, thanking it for all it taught me about life and how not to live it?

Realistically, I'd probably get the hell out of there and leave it to be dealt to by a SWAT team, but that doesn't seem anywhere near as therapeutic. Unlike the criminals in the world around us, those wreaking havoc between our ears won't ever have to pay a price for the pain and suffering they cause. Whether it's depression, bipolar, anxiety, or my old mate anorexia, the world's most prolific criminals continue getting away with generations of abuse unpunished, never brought to justice by the court of law, forever free to ruin billions of innocent lives without consequence.

If that seems unfair, it's because when it comes to mental illness, life is unfair. Believe me, no number of sadistic thought experiments have made me feel like justice against anorexia has been served. Thinking of the illness as something separate from myself played a vital role in my recovery, but by doing this, all I was really doing was protecting myself from an unsettling truth: it was a creation of my brain, so in reality, that bully between my ears never existed. Not only will it never face the wrath of our legal system, but outside of my mind and imagination, it will never face any punishment at all.

This may seem rather morbid, but thankfully, I realised in 2017 that when it came to mental illness, there were two things I could do to get back at it for what it did to me: I could use what it taught me to become happier than ever before, and could share my experience to prevent others from falling into its trap. These options may not seem as vengeful as those offered by that thought experiment, but if my experience is anything to go by, they are no less therapeutic.

Happiness is any mental illness' worst enemy, so what better way to get my revenge than to make myself and those around me happier than if it had never entered my life? An internal sense of justice is all we can ask for, and by using my experience with mental illness to work against itself, I realised I had the potential to achieve that in spades.

***

In 2017, I went a long way toward getting the revenge against anorexia that I craved. Not only did I make it through my final year of high school alive, but less than three years since leaving the psych ward, I did it in the most anti-anorexic way possible: by becoming happier than ever before, heavier than ever before, and by sharing what the illness taught me with as many people as I could.

At the start of that year, I was lucky enough to be voted as my school's head boy. This wasn't something I was expecting, and if I'm being honest, part of me wondered whether I was ready to take on that kind of responsibility. Alongside the deputy head boy, Nathan, and twenty-four other prefects, this meant I had to spend the year setting the best example I could for the rest of the school, and if possible, having some kind of lasting influence on its younger students.

My mental health may have been better than ever, but with 1200 students and 80 staff now tracking my 'success', I knew keeping it that way would be another challenge altogether. For the past two years, I'd been putting as little pressure on myself as possible, yet now here I was with what felt like the weight of the whole school on my shoulders. I could try as hard as I liked to take that pressure off, but there was no escaping the fact that head boy was a make-or-break role, so unlike the last couple of years, failure simply wouldn't be an option.

Thankfully, not only did I prevent my mental health from slipping, but with more external pressure on me than ever before, I found a way to let it thrive. Being head boy may have been an important role, but the way I saw it, nothing was more important than maintaining – and, if possible, improving – my already healthy state of mind.

Yes, there were expectations that the grades I achieved, the speeches I made and the overall examples I set were of the highest standard, but by putting my mental health first, I knew I was putting myself in the best position I could to reach them. It was a case of minimising what that external pressure did to my internal state of mind, and through doing so, becoming the happiest – and most successful – version of head boy that I could be.

For the majority of that year, only Rob, my close mates and some former teachers were aware that I had anorexia as a younger student. Of them, I'd imagine only Rob was aware I'd been battling it until the year before. The rest of the school was either completely oblivious or, for those who knew me back in Year Nine or Ten, under the impression I'd had time off school for problems with my heart. Hardly anyone knew that I'd spent time in a psych ward, and aside from Rob and those close to my family, no one knew how close I'd come to losing my life.

Keeping this information private wasn't necessarily my intention, but if I'm being honest, part of me did feel proud to have 'faked' having my shit together for so long when I didn't. I've also never been the biggest extrovert, and at an all-boys school in the 2010s, opportunities to share what I'd been through never seemed to arise naturally in conversation.

There was more mental health awareness than there used to be, but keeping my story private still well and truly seemed like the most sensible option. I knew that battling (and beating) anorexia was nothing to be ashamed of, but I still wasn't entirely sure that others would think the same.

This made it a pretty big deal when one day near the end of that year, I decided to share my story not only with my mates, but the entire school at the same time.

***

The rest of Napier Boys' assumed it would be like any other Monday assembly. We'd sing the national anthem and the school song, the headmaster would make a speech, I'd help him hand out certificates, and a prefect would read a few inspirational quotes. Then everyone would stand, the staff would leave the hall, and the students would hear the daily notices before being dismissed to interval. In more ways than one, this assembly broke the mould.

Only Rob, the headmaster and his deputy knew that I'd be the one making the speech that day, and of them, only Rob had read the speech in advance. For everyone else packed into that hall, my speech came as a complete surprise, not just because I was the one making it, but for the vast majority of those listening, because of what I said.

For the very first time, I admitted to the outside world that I, Harry Averill, had battled a mental illness, and as embarrassed and emasculated as I felt to share it, that the name of that illness was anorexia.

October 2017

I'm going to be honest with you, men. What I'm about to talk about isn't something I really want to talk about, nor is it something any of you probably want to hear.

In fact, I was pretty close to pulling the pin on this whole idea. I thought maybe I'd be better off talking about honesty or integrity or something like that – as I do during Friday assemblies.

I worried about how you'd respond to what I'm about to say. Whether you'd take it all the wrong way – make a joke of it – because sometimes that's what boys do when they don't want to face the reality of a situation.

But then I thought, nah, this is Napier Mens'. We know what's right and what's wrong. We know when it's time to be serious and when it's time to throw around a bit of friendly banter. We know all about the word respect, and we know when to use it.

Well, men, this is one of those serious times, and I'm trusting you all to listen and treat what I'm about to say with respect and give it the time of day it deserves because, as I said, this isn't something I feel comfortable talking about, and I know this isn't something a lot of you will feel comfortable hearing. And that – the fact we don't talk about it – is exactly what we need to change.

So if you haven't picked it up already, I'm talking about mental health. Or, as I like to call it, mind health. Because I, as well as anyone, know the stigma associated with the words 'mental health' these days. We hear it all the time in the media, and we're all aware of that horrible stigma attached to it – especially amongst young men like you and me.

And to be honest, I find that stigma pretty stupid. In fact, I think the stigma associated with mental health may just be more dangerous than mental illness itself.

So let's not call it mental health, because I think it is associated with a few too many negative ideas. Today, let's call it mind health – the healthiness of your conscience, and the friendliness of that voice inside your head.

At this point, I know some of you will be wondering what I'm going on about – you'll be thinking this speech is getting a bit too airy-fairy.

I'm aware of that and believe me, I used to feel exactly the same way about this kind of thing.

I actually remember in Year Nine, instead of going to prep one night, a guy came into the hostel and talked to us about mind health. I, as did most people, just sat there, didn't take anything in, and left the same person I was when I arrived. Everything just went in one ear and out the other.

I think that's often how young men like us treat these things – like we're bulletproof. We're always thinking we're the lucky ones – the ones who'll never have to worry about getting seriously sick, be that physically or mentally sick.

And that's the way it should be – after all, being optimistic is a big part of being happy. But that doesn't mean we shouldn't be prepared in case one day, things do go wrong.

You see, I'd only ever gone to the doctors a few times as a kid and could count on one hand how many sick days I'd had. In fact, just before I started here, my parents got a letter from the doctors asking if I still lived in the area because they hadn't seen me for so long. I was genuinely oblivious to the fact that I could get sick, let alone mentally sick.

Yet three years ago, I did get sick – really sick. It was like one day, I just caught a bug, and this bug got inside my brain and eventually turned me into a completely different person.

Within months, I went from a happy, healthy Year Nine to someone so riddled with anorexia that I couldn't bring myself to eat, and felt like I had to exercise every minute of every day; someone so depressed that I questioned whether my life was worth living anymore, and wondered if the world was better off without me; someone so mentally and physically unwell that for parts of Year Nine and Ten, I lived in a psychiatric hospital.

I know that's deep, and probably a bit too deep for a Monday morning. I know to some of you that seems unrealistic, as do I, even after going through it all myself.

But unfortunately, that's the nature of the beast, men. You'll never appreciate the bliss of having a healthy mind until you have an unhealthy one. You'll never know how quickly things can change until they do.

And it's weird, but even when I was at my sickest – even when I was in hospital after almost starving and exercising myself to death – I still didn't have the sense to talk to others about what was going on inside my head.

Even then, I was too embarrassed to be honest about the things I was feeling and the thoughts I was having. I still thought I was bulletproof – that I could push through the pain and figure it all out on my own.

To this day, that's something I really do regret. You see, the only way to make yourself better when something like that happens is by sharing with others what's really going on.

My inability to swallow my pride and take down those walls of 'manliness' by admitting to others I needed help almost cost me my life, and it took away years of my life that I'll never get back.

If only I'd had the balls to ask for help right at the very start – right when I sensed something upstairs wasn't quite right – I would never have had to go through what I did and would have never had to work as hard as I did to get my life back on track.

It all comes from that stigma I talked about before. So many of us are under the impression that admitting to the struggles inside our heads shows weakness. So many of us feel that sharing something like that with our mates or family makes us a lesser person – less like the staunch, emotionless male stereotype adopted by the generations before us.

Men, that is so far from the truth. You see, the bravest thing I ever did was accept that things inside my head needed to change, and accept that I couldn't make those changes on my own. In fact, of all the things I've done in my life, that was what required the most balls. It may just be the manliest thing I've ever done.

Yet every day, young men – no different to you or me – lose their lives simply because they are too ashamed or embarrassed to ask for the help they need. Like it or not, that's something we need to change.

So let's remove the stigma, because it's ultimately up to us – the next generation – to be the change this society needs. Let's take this matter into our own hands and turn the tide of something that has cost the lives of far too many good young men.

Ridiculing those battling a mental illness is not manliness. Failing to be the one who's there for your mate to talk to is not manliness. Keeping a mental illness to yourself – believe it or not, that's not manliness, either.

So let's redefine what it means to be manly, because if you really are for the boys, you'll make sure all the boys are okay, and you'll tell the boys when you're not.

Something as simple as 'Bro, you all good?' when one of the boys has dropped his bottom lip – that's manly. Something as simple as 'Bro,

I'm not all good' when you're not feeling too flash yourself – that's manly. Looking out for your mates and getting yourself the mates that look out for you – that's manly.

And if you are one of those good men struggling at the moment, remember, you are not alone. Whether it's your mates, your family, Mr Silver – whoever you feel most comfortable talking to – if you're out there and your thoughts are keeping you in a dark place, be brave, be manly, and ask for help.

Because it's all good to not feel all good, but it's not all good to keep it to yourself.

No soldier goes to war without an army. We all have our battles, but that doesn't mean we have to face them alone.

To this day, I've never been more nervous before making a speech. I think I knew deep down that it would be well received, but I also knew that almost everyone in that hall, for better or worse, would never look at me the same again.

By making that speech, I was publicly stamping anorexia to my identity, so although I made it clear that I'd beaten it, how was I to know how people's perceptions of me would change? Would it make some students think I'm less of a man? Would it make some regret voting for me as head boy? Would it make some of my mates feel awkward around me?

I guess I'll never know the answers to those questions, but if one thing is for sure, making that speech is the best thing I've ever done. As well as sparking more mind health conversations and encouraging others to get the help they need, on a personal level, it felt like an almighty finger pull to the mental illness of my past. Having the self-assurance to take that risk and share my story was vengeful enough, but by doing so, I felt like I finally gave anorexia the public stoning it deserved.

That bully was now dead and insignificant somewhere deep within my mind, but after making that speech, I imagined it turning in its grave as it realised what a happy and positive legacy it had left behind.

***

By the end of the school year, I was ten kilos heavier than I was when I started. This wasn't because I let the stress of head boy get to me, nor was it because at eighteen years old, I discovered beer for the first time. Believe it or not, neither of those statements is true.

The real reason I put on weight that year was because I wanted to. I've mentioned before that I wanted to distance myself from anorexia as much as I could. Well, aside from using what it taught me to become happier and helping others to do the same, I decided there was no better way to do that than by putting on weight for the sake of it. Anorexia is best known for making its victims skinny and weak. For that reason alone, I wanted to bulk up and get strong.

At the start of that year, my weight was right where BMI charts said it should be for someone of my age, height, and sex. I could have done with the extra kilos if I was still playing rugby, but after concussions forced me to stop that the previous season, this reasoning no longer applied.

I knew another ten kilos would change how I looked, but by this point, I was old and wise enough to know that appearance wasn't a healthy obsession to have. When it came down to it, my only incentive to put on weight was to prove to myself (and anorexia) that – contrary to what I used to believe – nothing terrible would happen if I did.

For the entire year, I ate as much food as time and stomach capacity gave room for, and when my mates went to rugby training after school, I went to the hostel gym. As with any exercise, I only pushed myself as hard as my enjoyment allowed, but with time, the weights I was lifting felt lighter, and the body I was using felt stronger. I'd already taught myself to think of food as fuel, yet now that I was seeing it work to my advantage, I was learning to think of it as a friend.

Reaching that ten-kilo goal was a great feeling, even if it did come with a few unsettling comments about my changing appearance. I knew that no one was trying to offend me, but as a former anorexic, hearing how much bigger I looked certainly took some getting used to.

These comments initially all came across as insults, but I soon learned how to desensitise myself to them, and by the end of the year, I could interpret them all as compliments. I knew anything anorexia made me stress over was something that worked against my state of mind, so the way I saw it, the less I cared about things like body fat percentage, caloric content, and exercise intensity, the better my life would be.

For this reason, when I finished high school at the end of 2017, not only was I double the weight I'd been back in 2013, but thanks to anorexia, I was also double the man.

Eighteen

THE NEXT CHAPTER

Mental illness isn't good for much, but if my experience is anything to go by, it leaves you with much more than just a weird story to tell. It also leaves you with one of the world's most valuable assets – the right approach to life. I wouldn't wish what I went through on my worst enemy, yet at the same time, I'll always be grateful to have gone through what I did at such a young age. Life is all about perspective, and sometimes living with the wrong one is what it takes to find the one that sets you free.

It's now almost five years since I finished high school, and that makes it almost ten years since I crossed the line between childhood and what I thought was growing up. A lot has happened since crossing that line, some of it good, some of it bad, but on the whole, I think the younger version of me would consider the journey a success. It got off to the worst possible start, and the route taken was remarkably different to what I had planned, but looking back, it's hard not to feel like everything happened the way it was meant to.

When it comes down to it, all I've ever wanted in life is to be happy. My 2013 track record may suggest otherwise, but all that's ever changed has been the timescale I've had in mind to achieve it.

As a kid, I focused mainly on how happy I was in the moment, and thanks to the adults paying the bills and keeping me in line, this approach was sustainable. Aside from the odd fitness training for rugby and those dreaded cross-country days, my enjoyment formed the basis of almost every decision I made.

In an ideal world, we'd all be able to spend our whole lives this way, doing only what we love with the freedom to avoid almost anything we don't. We'd continue following our childhood instincts, always putting today's happiness ahead of tomorrow's without the world ever bringing us back down to size. Our expenses would continue to be paid, our relationships would continue to flourish, and no matter what eating and exercise habits we developed in a consequence-free world, all aspects of our health would continue to thrive.

As nice as that world would be, we all know it's not the one we live in. In the real world, there's no such thing as a free lunch, and for all their progress, scientists still haven't figured out how we can have our cakes and eat them too. Focusing on your immediate happiness may be the best strategy if you're a privileged kid like I was, but long-term, it's a sure-fire way to go broke, lose friends, and put your health at serious risk.

It would be great if this weren't the case, but we haven't evolved for a life of endless pleasure, and there's a reason for that. How much we enjoy today has a direct impact on how much we can enjoy tomorrow, and because of that, getting the most happiness out of adulthood requires strategy, sacrifice, and in general, a more long-term approach. At the crux of it, it's a balancing act between enjoying today, and building yourself the platform for happier tomorrows.

As the first few chapters of this book explained, I got that balance seriously wrong as a thirteen-year-old kid, and this made my mind a breeding ground for anorexia. After thirteen years of putting my immediate happiness first, I arrived at high school and, for some reason or another, I thought I had to switch straight to the opposite extreme.

Suddenly, how happy I felt today became irrelevant, and everything I did was an attempt to build the perfect life for myself, not tomorrow or the next day, but someday far into the future. I didn't know when that day would come, just that being successful was the only way for me to get there and that when I did, I would forever be happy. One day it would all be worth it, but until that day, success, not happiness, had to come first.

Of course, the day of perpetual happiness never arrived, and even if it did, sacrificing years of happiness just so your eventual success brings it back hardly seems sensible. Luckily for me, it only took a year of rather severe unhappiness to realise that. Running entered my life, anorexia hijacked my mind, and my long-term approach to happiness transformed into an almost deadly quest for success.

A long-term approach to life may be necessary to build a career, sustain relationships and keep on top of your health, but when it comes to happiness, an immediate to short-term approach makes a lot more sense. I believe that anything worth achieving can be done with a healthy state of mind, and if that's not possible – if your long-term goals are making you unhappy for a sustained period – I'd argue that what you're trying to achieve isn't necessary. It's as simple as that.

Besides, if my experience is anything to go by, a healthy state of mind is what enables success, not the other way around. The more clearheaded and happy we are upstairs, the more productive, likeable, and healthy – in other words, the more successful – we can be. That may sound too good to be true, but if there's one thing my journey has taught me, it's that it isn't.

***

Finding the right perspective is one thing, but in a world of constant change, holding on to it is another. I'd learned a lot about life by the time I finished school, but by no means did I have it all figured out. Like anyone, I still had – and still have – a lot to learn about life and how to get the most happiness from it that I can.

After spending my life on the east coast of the North Island, the following year, I made the move to the University of Otago. I'd heard great things about the student culture down there, and after so long in Hawke's Bay, I liked the idea of spreading my wings and putting as much distance between me and familiarity as possible.

I had a few ideas about what I wanted to study, but it took five degree changes and plenty of soul-searching for me to settle on the Commerce and Science degree I finished last year. The problem wasn't that I couldn't find what interested me, but like a lot of people, that I was too interested in far too many things.

I'd always seen myself in the business world, but after going through what I did, I also yearned to learn more about the mind and how to help others with theirs. In the end, the economics and psychology majors I settled on gave me the best of both worlds. Going forward, I hope to dabble in both as best I can.

The thing about Uni is, almost everyone is there to create a better future for themselves, yet never in our lives will there be more opportunities to let loose and enjoy the perks of adulthood. Like most students, I struggled to find the sweet spot between having fun today, feeling happy (not hungover or 'hanxious') tomorrow, and building myself the platform for a happier future. There's a fine line between getting the grades you need and having the most fun you can, and no matter what side of the equation I chose, I felt like I was selling myself short.

For one, there was a semester where I put too much pressure on myself academically, and as a result, I didn't enjoy myself anywhere near as much as I should have. I let the pressures of the outside world seep into my internal state of mind, and before I knew it, I was back with the same 'no pain, no gain' approach that caused me so much trouble in the past. It didn't take long for my mind health to deteriorate, and as you might expect, my results in the classroom quickly followed suit.

Letting this happen may seem silly after everything I'd been through, but like anyone, I'm easily influenced by the behaviour of those around me. Universities are full of competitive people with lofty long-term goals, and as hard as I tried to keep my priorities in check, I eventually got sucked into their rat race for success. A familiar darkness returned, pessimistic thoughts gained traction within my mind, and before I knew it, the world around me appeared in much darker tones.

Thankfully, I had the awareness to realise what the problem was, and by sharing with others what was going on, I went a long way toward solving it. I was flatting with ten of my good mates at the time, and after opening up to them one night at dinner, they started giving me all the support I needed to turn things around. Whether checking in over a beer or going for a walk and talk with me around the block, they responded like all good mates should.

They reaffirmed to me the wonders of being open about these things, and the importance of surrounding yourself with the type of people who care.

Within a couple of months, I was back feeling happier than ever and had pulled myself out of what, for some people, would have been a dangerous downward spiral. It was a close call, but a timely reminder of what's most important and another massive kick in the guts to the mental illness of my past.

When I wasn't putting too much pressure on myself academically, like most Otago students, I spent a lot of time putting too much pressure on my liver. Rather than neglecting my current state of mind, this was a case of going too far the other way – getting carried away on the beers at the expense of my happiness in the days that followed. I didn't drink anywhere near as much as some people, but looking back, I did make it harder on my state of mind than I needed to.

After everything I'd been through, you'd think I'd know better than to put myself through the 'hanxiety' of a hangover, but then again, some of my best memories were made on nights I regretted the next day. I don't always make the right decisions, and after a few beers, I often make the wrong ones. Yet the way I see it, it's not about being perfectly rational but being as happy as I can as often as I can, and learning from the times I get that balance wrong. Whether this eventually leads to sobriety, a few beers after work, or occasionally pushing the boat out too far, each time I get that balance wrong, I get closer to living the life that works best for me.

Clearly, I've still got a lot to learn about life and how best to live it. Getting the most happiness out of each day is hard enough. Getting the most happiness out of life probably takes a lot longer than one lifetime to figure out. The world around me will never stop changing, nor will my place within it. This means that, like anyone, all I can do is try to be – and never stop believing I can be – happier than I am now.

As for my future, I don't know what's in store for me any more than the next guy. I don't know what direction my career will take, whether I'll get married or have kids, nor do I know whether I'll live to a ripe old age or get hit by a bus tomorrow. I don't know what cards I'll be dealt next, and I certainly don't know who's up there dealing them.

What I do know, is that when it comes to how happy my life will be, how I play my cards will determine a hell of a lot more than which ones I'm dealt. For that reason, I know that no matter what happens, I'll never stop *trying* to be happier, I'll never forget what mental illness taught me, and with a bit of luck, I'll never stop helping others write better 'next chapters' of their own.

As long as I can do that, I'll consider this life a success.

Holidaying in Taupō a couple of months after leaving the psych ward.

With my hostel mates, Campbell and Flynn (right), snagging a picture with Kiwi legend, Mark Richardson, back in 2015.

Head boy mugshot, 2017.

At my final school ball with the rest of the prefects team. I'm second from right at the front.

With Grandad, Mum, Dad, Granny and Papa after my final school prizegiving.

Enjoying the Dunedin nightlife on St Patrick's Day, 2018.

Having a beer on the beach with some of my Arana College mates. I'm second from right at the back.

With my second-year flat mates outside our Castle Street flat.

Balling with a couple of university mates, Georgia and Sophie, back in 2019.

With four of my ten flat mates during my third year. As if that wasn't enough, the following year there were twelve of us.

Oscar (left), Jack, Dad, Mum and me at a cousin's wedding last year.

With my current Hawke's Bay flatmates: Campbell (right), Maddie, and Georgia.

THANKS

It takes a village to raise a child and a lot more than that to raise one with a mental illness. I could never thank everyone who made this book possible, but the following is my attempt to scratch the surface.

Thank you, first and foremost, to the health professionals who saved my life between 2013 and 2015. To my long-serving GP, Nicola McKendry, my CAFS team (especially Dr Henk Verhulst), the staff at Hastings Hospital, the staff and fellow patients at the Regional Rangatahi Adolescent Inpatient Service, Victoria Marsden, and James Knight, thank you for helping me beat what could have been a life-defining illness.

You had the unfortunate task of dealing with me at my worst, and you did it with more compassion, understanding and patience than the anorexic version of me deserved. I will never forget you, and I will forever be grateful that you gave me a second chance in life.

To Michelle Deed, Sharon Dudding, and Linda Nel, thank you for your kindness and flexibility as I transitioned back to mainstream education and for all you did to make it as stress-free as my stressed-out brain allowed. I was able to return to 'normal' life in record-breaking time, and that was in no small part thanks to you.

To Murray Barker, Sharon Taylor, Bruce Smith, Rob Silver, and the rest of the Napier Boys' High School and Hostel staff, thank you for making my return to school possible and for everything you did to make it easier. I had some of the worst days of my life at that place, but thanks to you, I also had some of my best.

To the mates who stuck with me when I wasn't great company and all those I've made since, thank you for everything you've done to make me happier. I hope I can be as good to you as you've all been to me, and if you ever need somebody to talk to, know that I'll be there for you with open ears and arms.

To my aunties, uncles, cousins, family friends, and all those who supported my parents and me when times were tough, thank you for the meals you dropped off when I was in hospital, for all the cards, letters, and gifts you sent me, and for all the wines, beers and tears you shared with my parents during that time. A special thanks to the late Kim Harris (Big Harry): the only friend I let visit me in Hastings Hospital, and always one of my best supporters out of it. Your influence on me was the biggest when my life was darkest, yet I will always treasure those times we shared.

To Mum, Dad, Jack, Oscar, Granny, Papa, Gran, and Grandad, thank you for supporting me through thick and thin – through every hardship and every success. I hope I've made the rollercoaster I took you on worth every struggle. May I continue growing into the man you've always known I could be.

To Julie Dinneen, Tania Clifton-Smith, and Luke Elworthy, thank you for your invaluable editorial advice and for all the hard-earned tricks of the trade you've shared. Getting this thing published was always going to be a tough ask, but it was remarkably less so, thanks to you.

Last but certainly not least, thank you. I hope this book has been helpful in some way, or if nothing else, I hope it's been a tolerable way for you to pass the time. Check out my website (harryaverill.com) or Instagram (@harry_averill) to see where life takes me next, and if you're ever keen to get in touch, don't hesitate to flick me a message.

All the best, from my mind to yours.

GETTING HELP

If your mind ever makes you feel unsafe, please get in touch with your local mental health crisis team, or go to the emergency department of your nearest hospital.

If you or someone else is in immediate danger, phone 111 in New Zealand or 000 in Australia.

Other free and confidential support services are listed below. These are run by trained counsellors and volunteers. If you don't get the help you need the first time, please keep trying.

NEW ZEALAND

Eating Disorders Association of New Zealand: For eating disorder support, call 0800 2 EDANZ (0800 2 33269) or visit www.ed.org.nz for resources

Anxiety New Zealand: Call 0800 ANXIETY (0800 269 4389)

Depression Helpline: Call 0800 111 757, text 4202 or visit www.depression.org.nz for resources

Healthline: Call 0800 611 116

Kidsline: For young people up to 18 years of age, call 0800 KIDSLINE (0800 54 37 54)

Lifeline Aotearoa: Call 0800 LIFELINE (0800 543 354) or text HELP to 4357

National Mental Health Helpline: Call or text 1737

Parent Help: For caregivers seeking support, advice and practical strategies, call 0800 568 856

Rainbow Youth: Call (09) 376 4155

Rural Support Trust: Call 0800 787 254

Samaritans: Call 0800 726 666

Shine (Domestic Violence): Call 0508 744 633

Skylight: For support through trauma, loss, and grief, call 0800 299 100

Suicide Crisis Helpline: Call 0508 TAUTOKO (0508 828 865)

Supporting Families in Mental Illness: Call 0800 732 825

The Lowdown: Text 5626, email team@thelowdown.co.nz or visit thelowdown.co.nz for resources

What's Up: For 5-18 year olds, call 0800 942 8787 or visit what sup.co.nz for web chat and resources

Women's Refuge: Call 0800 733 843 (0800 REFUGE)

Youthline: Call 0800 376 633, text 234, email talk@youthline.co.nz or visit youthline.co.nz for web chat and resources

AUSTRALIA

Butterfly Foundation: For eating disorder support, call 1800 ED HOPE (1800 33 4673), email support@butterfly.org.au or visit butterfly.org.au for web chat and resources

1800 RESPECT: For those affected by sexual abuse or violence, phone 1800 RESPECT (1800 737 732) or visit 1800respect.org.au

Beyond Blue: For depression and anxiety support, call 1300 22 4636 or visit www.beyondblue.org.au

Headspace: For young people and their caregivers, call 1800 650 890 or visit headspace.org.au

Kids Helpline: For young people and their caregivers, call 1800 55 1800 or visit kidshelpline.com.au

Kidsline: For young people up to 18 years of age, call 1800 55 1800

Lifeline: Call 13 11 14

Suicide Callback Service: Call 1300 659 467 or visit suicidecall-backservice.org.au

USA

National Eating Disorders Association: For eating disorder support, call or text (800) 931-2237 or visit www.nationaleatingdisorders.org for web chat and resources

Crisis Text Line: Text HOME to 741741

Suicide Prevention Helpline: Call 1 800 273 8255

UK

Beat Eating Disorders: For eating disorder support, call 0808 801 0677 (England), 0808 801 0432 (Scotland), 0808 801 0433 (Wales), 0808 801 0434 (Northern Ireland), or visit www.beateatingdisorders.org.uk for resources

1 800 SUICIDE: Call 1 800 784 2433

1 800 273 TALK: Call 1 800 273 8255

Crisis Text Line: Text 85258

UK Suicide Hotline: Call 08 457 90 90 90

CANADA

National Eating Disorder Information Centre: For eating disorder support, call 1-866-NEDIC-20, email nedic@uhn.ca or visit nedic.ca for web chat and resources

Crisis Support: Call 1 833 456 4566

Crisis Text Line: Text HOME to 686868

www.ingramcontent.com/pod-product-compliance
Lightning Source LLC
Chambersburg PA
CBHW061344230926
51848CB00004B/525
9781991186706